THE MINORITY INTEREST

WOMEN WHO SUCCEED IN THE ACCOUNTANCY PROFESSION

THE MINORITY INTEREST

WOMEN WHO SUCCEED IN THE ACCOUNTANCY PROFESSION

Patricia Barker

Chartered
Accountants
Ireland

Published in 2009 by
Chartered Accountants Ireland
Chartered Accountants House
47-47 Pearse Street
Dublin 2

ISBN 978-0-903854-10-8

This publication is designed to provide accurate and authoritative information in regard to the subject matter covered. It is provided on the understanding that the ICAI is not engaged in rendering professional services. If professional advice or other expert assistance is required, the services of a competent professional should be sought.

Designed by Datapage, Dublin, Ireland
Printed by Turners Printing, Ireland

To Robert

CONTENTS

ACKNOWLEDGEMENTS

The author wishes to express her gratitude to the women partners in the Big Four firms who contributed to the research by completing the pilot questionnaire and by giving of their time, invaluable experience and considered views during the course of the interviews. Without them, this book would simply not have been possible. Many thanks also to the male partners who took part in the Focus Group.

The advice of Professor Kathy Monks of Dublin City University and Professor Eileen Drew of Trinity College, Dublin are also gratefully acknowledged, as is the assistance of James Brunton and Padraig Mac Giolla with the management of the data.

I would like to thank the Irish Accountancy Educational Trust for their support and encouragement.

Special thanks go to Michael Diviney, commissioning editor, for his tolerance, patient reading and good suggestions. I would particularly like to mention Michael's predecessor, Kieran Lyons (RIP) for his enthusiasm and good-natured intellectual challenge. Thanks also to Elizabeth MacAuley, and to Robert and Victoria Barker who proof read various versions of the text.

To all: *Go raibh míle maith agaibh go léir.*

PROLOGUE

My father was in deep discussion with Robin Lewis-Crosby, who was somewhat puzzled at the precise nature of the problem.

– I am at my wits' end to know what to do with her!
– Why don't you put her into the Bank?
– She's hellish poor at taking orders!
– Well, nursing then?
– She doesn't like blood and, anyway, she would baulk at the bed pans!
– The 'Service' then?
– She asks too many questions!
– What about one of these air hostesses?
– She hasn't got the looks!
– Well, for Pete's sake, Mac, what has she got?

My father sighed and settled down into the deep leather chair. Robin Lewis-Crosby poured them both another drink and reflected on how often he had to listen to tales of despair from his clients about their recalcitrant sons who resisted all efforts to settle them into a respectable career. This, however, was the first time the wayward offspring was a daughter, and he felt somewhat outside his comfort zone.

He and my Dad had both fought in the British Army during the Second World War. They had come back to Dublin to carve out professional careers for themselves after they had resigned their commissions in the late 1940s. Robin had become a partner in Stokes Bros. & Pim (later to become Stokes Kennedy Crowley and, later still, KPMG). My father was the Company Secretary in Williams & Woods, and Robin was their audit partner.

I had been making a living teaching sailing in Morocco. My respectable, middle-class father was appalled that I was 'keeping company' with a North American Indian, with thick shoulder-length black hair and a Black Panther tattoo on his wrist. He had deserted from the US Army in Vietnam and had a passing interest in the hash pods that grew in the Rif Mountains. My father had concluded that it was time I was brought back to Dublin and 'persuaded' to do something sensible with my life.

My money ran out when the wind died and the autumn closed in. Tourist numbers were dwindling and there were fewer customers for sailing lessons. The small number who could be persuaded to try sailing were quickly put off by the slack winds and the mill-pond conditions, which were more likely to induce sea sickness than adrenalin. I sent a telegram home requesting a small loan. The response from my Dad was a one-way ticket back to Dublin. Unbeknownst to me, he had arranged to meet Robin to seek his advice. I looked at the airline ticket and my empty purse and, as my empty stomach rumbled, I reconciled myself to a temporary return home to work somewhere and save up enough money to return to my life of freedom.

Back home, I sat back contentedly, replete on one of my mother's steak and kidney puddings. I contemplated the Ireland I had returned to. It was 1968 and the general societal expectation of girls leaving school was that we would teach, join the Bank or the Civil Service, or do nursing. We might go to university, provided we had Latin and Maths in the Leaving Certificate and had obtained three honours. In reality, however, these routes were just temporary backwaters on which we were to paddle gently until we had identified, hooked and landed a suitable husband. We were expected to be flashing a diamond by the time we were 23 years of age. My mother, who had been a serving nursing officer in the British Army during the war, had nursed my father when he was wounded in Burma. She had given up her career to marry my father and rear three children. In accepting his proposal of marriage, she probably had little inkling what life would be like for a Protestant Englishwoman in the Dublin of the 1940s. The social attitudes underpinned by the marriage bar meant that she had to give up her career and devote herself to housewifely and motherly duties. She filled the post efficiently, but restlessly. I still have childhood recollections of lying in bed, supposedly fast asleep, listening to my parents' muffled discussions about the role of women in the home. She caused a nine-day wonder in our street when she went back to work while we were still at school. My father wore a wounded face for months as he tried in vain to find any evidence that my mother could not manage the household, the children, his needs and her very demanding job. She undoubtedly influenced me to question the received wisdom about the role of women in Irish society.

That afternoon, back in 1968, she warned me that my Dad was due to meet with Robin and would probably present me with some solution to my 'problem'. I loved my father dearly and understood his desire to see me happy, settled, and snuggled into the cosy nest that all girls were assumed to desire for themselves. Dad thought I was wonderful and could do anything I wanted. He mistakenly believed that I was a mathematical genius because I always did well at Maths in my all-girl school, where my peers, if they ever had any interest in Maths, had it firmly sucked out of them at an early stage by an educational system that assumed that honours Maths and science were for boys! My father thought I was so wonderful (albeit a trifle undisciplined) that I could become a Chartered Accountant and could usefully be articled to Mr Lewis-Crosby.

Robin Lewis-Crosby, on the other hand, was not convinced that I was wonderful. He did not view the prospect of having a female articled clerk, especially one like me, with great enthusiasm. My father persuaded me to go and speak with him, which I did. Robin made it very clear that he and my father had come up with the idea of offering me Articles of Clerkship since I really seemed to be unsuited for any of the normal 'girls' jobs'. He scanned my best clothes (a very tight pair of ice blue jeans, a pink embroidered kaftan and high boots) with a liverish eye and suggested that I might need to invest in a plainer costume if I were to join the firm.

In my favour, my father was a client and I was an Anglican. In those days, there were very few Roman Catholics in SB&P. Since I was good at maths, he suggested that I might be up to doing some of the shoebox accounting jobs, and maybe a little ticking and totting. This sounded excruciating to me and my attention began to drift. Robin mused that, by the end of my first year, it was possible that I might like to review my situation. What he actually meant was that I would surely have found a prudent, respectable young man and could then retire to breed. In fact, he was a complete gentleman and very charming, but the message between the lines was clear: the accountancy profession was an unusual, although not impossible, place for a lady. It was, however, heavily populated by eligible young men and surely, in spite of my plain looks and my unladylike spiritedness, I would find a suitable boy. I almost completely switched off! He went on to explain kindly that, with a 73% failure rate in the accountancy examinations, it was difficult enough for young men to pass, and it would be extraordinarily difficult for a young lady to succeed. It was at this point in the conversation that I sat up and became engaged.

> – Are you saying that, because I am a girl, I couldn't pass the exams?
> – Well, only 15 ladies have passed the exams in the 50 years since ladies were admitted to the Institute.
> – OK. Where do I sign? When can I start?

And so began a career in accountancy, at a most exciting and challenging time as the profession was beginning to open up to women. Stokes Bros. & Pim gave me an excellent training and first class experience in a wide range of audit, tax and special project assignments. I was very happy with them and although I think they thought I was a bit on the wild side, they rose to the challenge and treated me well - just the same as the male articled clerks. I did pass the exams and qualified before my period of articles expired. I also found a suitable boy!

The experience of being one of the early women entrants to the profession of Chartered Accountancy has led to an interest in the progression of women in this previously all-male territory. That interest led to the research which is described in the chapters that follow.

1

♦

NO PLACE FOR A LADY

I signed my Articles of Indenture in 1968 with Stokes Bros. & Pim and thus began a career in the accountancy profession which has spanned 40 years. There were no other women articled clerks in the firm at the time and there was only one other girl in the lectures for the professional examinations. The pioneering experience of being virtually the only female working on many of the assignments and projects I undertook was exhilarating, challenging and sometimes terrifying. My specialism has been in technical financial reporting, but I have always had an interest in the role of women and in the gradual inclusion of women in this most male of environments. Now, in 2009, women in Ireland enter the accountancy profession in equal numbers to men. But their representation in the elite positions at the top of the profession is less than 20 per cent, which is similar to the statistics in other English-speaking countries. This is partly attributable to the obstacles that women encounter as they progress up the ranks of the profession; and partly due to the fact that women are more likely than men to decide to 'quit' the partnership track. Whatever the cause, however, it is more difficult for women than men to attain and retain elite positions. This has implications for the women who aspire to achieve these positions, and for the accountancy profession that seeks diversity in its leadership.

Looking back over the past 40 years prompts reflections on the genesis and development of the entry of women into a profession that was originally constructed by men, for men, to serve the needs of male clients. Whether you are: a woman accountant; someone working with or employing women accountants; a parent of a daughter who might become an accountant; a teacher of students who have entered or may enter accountancy; or someone who has just picked up this book by accident, I invite you to explore with me the story of the admission of women into this most male of bastions; consider the profile of elite women who have overcome all the barriers to progress to the very top of the profession; and contemplate future policies that might tip the balance and encourage more women through the portals of the elite chambers of accountancy.

OBJECTIVES OF THIS BOOK

The chapters that follow describe the struggle that Irish women had to undertake in order to gain access to the professions and, in particular, to the accountancy profession. The disparity between the proportion of women entering the accountancy profession and the proportion of women holding elite positions will be considered. This book will focus on exploring this disparity, not from the negative perspective of why women *do not* achieve elite positions, but through the more positive lens of why some women *do* achieve those positions. While the obstacles and barriers are pertinent and cannot be ignored, I will concentrate more on what is needed to overcome them. The intention is, therefore, not to wallow in the miseries and injustices surrounding the exclusion of women, but rather to try to identify common characteristics of those women who have succeeded in being included and to see if any lessons can be derived. The specific objectives of the book are, thus:

- To set the context of a profession that was developed for men and by men, and which gradually admitted women.
- To review the obstacles that women experienced and still experience in the context of the historical development of their admission to the profession and to review their greater propensity to 'quit'.
- To hear the voices and stories of women who have attained and retained elite positions and to consider common themes.
- To provide recommendations for future policy and procedures within the professional firms to facilitate the development of a better gender balance in the elite positions in accountancy.

LIMITATIONS

The focus here is on the themes emerging from the experiences of women who have succeeded in reaching partnership in the 'Big Four' firms (Deloitte, Ernst & Young, KPMG and PricewaterhouseCoopers – see Key Terms and Definitions below). Invariably, of course, there are other elements to career progression within the profession that are not considered. Those specific limitations are defined below.

- There are features of achieving elite positions that are common to men and women. These include high-level technical competence, leadership qualities, loyalty, and skill at bringing clients to the firm. These are all considered when a business case is being made for any candidate for partnership, regardless of gender. This book is limited to those qualities that are different for women and does not address the common qualities.
- The literature on women in accountancy identifies barriers and obstacles that women encounter. It is assumed, since there is no evidence to the contrary, that such obstacles are unique to women. However, it seems possible that some of those obstacles may apply to some men (for example, men who have a desire to be more involved with the rearing of their children). This book makes no attempt to test this issue, although it may prove fruitful ground for further study.
- The evidence for my empirical study of the elite women reported in Chapter 4 was initially gathered from the women partners in Irish Big Four firms. This is a small population, so it was extended to women partners in the same Big Four firms in the English-speaking business economies. The policies and practices of Big Four firms are largely homogeneous and, although there was potential for some cultural differences, none was detected in the analysis of the data. Forty-three women partners in Big Four firms were interviewed. They did not represent a random sample, or indeed, any kind of sample of the international partnerships. They were partners who could be personally introduced to me or who were personally known to me. Although not having a random sample may appear to be a limitation, it was at least partially overcome by conducting a large number of interviews. Additionally,

although all the interviewees were not Irish, no detectable cultural or other variations emerged, so the sample may be taken as being relatively bias free and providing good evidence.

- Apart from a small focus group, no interviews were conducted with male partners. Therefore, I can offer no comparisons with the themes that might arise for men. However, this may provide good research grounds in the future.

KEY TERMS AND DEFINITIONS

For the purposes of this book, the following key terms and definitions have been used:

- **Elite Women in Accountancy:** women who have attained partnership in a Big Four accountancy practice and who have remained for two years or longer.
- **Big Four Accountancy practice:** The four major worldwide accountancy practices, i.e. KPMG, PricewaterhouseCoopers, Deloitte and Ernst & Young.
- **The firm:** The Big Four accountancy practice.
- **Partner:** Professional accountancy practices are structured as partnerships and not as limited liability companies. A partner is an owner who is jointly and severally regarded as the owner of the assets of the partnership and responsible for all liabilities with no limitation.

STRUCTURE OF THE BOOK

This book is set out in six chapters:

Chapter 2 considers the historical context to women's struggle to gain the right to enter the accountancy profession and traces that struggle from the early nineteenth century to the present day.

Chapter 3 defines elite women in business, specifically in accountancy, and considers the emphasis the literature has placed on the barriers that women have encountered. It raises the issue of 'flight' and the propensity of women, more than men, to 'quit' or leave the partnership track.

Chapter 4 invites the reader to focus on the positive. It outlines the research methodology used and describes the conversations with elite women in the profession, deriving common themes from their stories that might explain why some women succeed in attaining and retaining elite positions in accountancy. The chapter outlines the interviewees' common personal characteristics and backgrounds.

Chapter 5 describes how the women managed their careers and dealt with the barriers and obstacles they encountered.

Chapter 6 analyses the findings and suggests recommendations arising from the conclusions reached for potential women partner candidates, for the firms and for the elite women themselves.

2

◆

THE STRUGGLE FOR ADMISSION
TO THE PROFESSION

The Eighteenth Century Perception of a Woman's Role

Until the 1920s, the accountancy profession was completely populated by men. Today, some 90 years later, there is complete and equal
freedom for women to enter the profession, but it is still difficult for
them to progress to the very top.

The right of entry for women, in 1919, into all the professions
was a hard won prize. To understand the story of this struggle for
equality, we must travel back a little in time. The debate about
women's place in society in general goes right back to the Greek
and Roman civilizations when women's role was mainly to be
decorative and to look after domestic matters. Fast-forwarding to
the 1700s, we observe considerable debate about 'the woman question' which dealt with women's mission and the seat of their power
and influence.[1] In the mid-1770s, John Gregory reminded his
daughters that women's role in life is to "soften the hearts and polish [the] manners of men".[2] Men were the important members of
society: the bread-winners, the warriors and the decision-makers.
However, left to their own devices, they could be crude and rough.
The thinking was that it was women's role to polish the rough sur-
faces and teach them the rules of polite society. This role of putting
manners on their menfolk was later extended by the acknowledge-
ment that genteel women could also influence men's actions by
persuading them to consider matters of relationship, behaviour
towards others and feelings. For example, in 1794, Fordyce reas-
sured young women that a:

... principal source of your importance is the very great and extensive influence which you in general have with our sex. ... There is an influence, there is an empire which belongs to you ... I mean that which has the heart as its object.[3]

In 1798, Thomas Gisborne reflected that women could extend their influence beyond the domestic and familial spheres into the public sphere. He referred to the complaints of young women that their days were filled with trivia and that men denied them the opportunity to utilise fully their intellectual capacities:

... the sphere of domestic life ... admits far less diversity of action and consequently of temptation, than is found in the widely differing professions and employments [of men].[4]

This period marked the beginnings of the further extension of a woman's role from the influencing and cultivation of her family in the private sphere to that of contributing to philanthropic and altruistic works of mercy in the public sphere. There appears to have been considerable debate about the role of middle-class women in the early 1800s and some women experienced anxiety about their status and what should be regarded as proper work for them. Most writers – and it should be recalled that the vast majority of writers were men – were very clear that, while women had influence, they did not have power. For example, in 1841, the editor of the *Edinburgh Review* rejected any equality for men and women in the affairs of state and the professions, warning that:

If women were ever made ostensibly powerful ... the spirit of chivalry ... would speedily cease. Women have immense influence ... [which] must be allowed to flow in its natural channels, namely domestic ones.[5]

Indeed, some women were themselves hesitant about the possibility of moving into the public sphere. In 1845, Sarah Ellis noted:

... women, in their position in life, must be content to be inferior to men: but as their inferiority consists chiefly in their want of power, this deficiency is abundantly made up to them by their capability of exercising influence.[6]

In April of 1850, Elizabeth Gaskell confessed to Tottie Fox that:

> ... *the discovery of one's exact work in the world is the puzzle ... I*
> *am sometimes coward enough to wish we were back in the darkness*
> *where obedience was the only seen duty of women.*[7]

J. Newton refers to this nineteenth century valorisation of women's influence as in the best interests of the men who proposed it. To have influence, she suggests, the middle-class woman was urged to relinquish self-definition and any desire for power and was urged to become identified only by her service to others, particularly to men.[8]

Beginnings of a role for women in the public sphere

In 1874, Isabella Tod, the pioneering activist in the cause of Irish women throughout the nineteenth century, suggested that the search for 'gentility' blinded parents to possible hardship for unmarried daughters who were left without appropriate qualification and means to secure their independence. She decried the condemnation of middle-class women to a decorative and useless role in society.[9] But, in spite of her protestations, the acquisition of accomplishments and a contribution to philanthropy were still regarded as more desirable than professional qualifications. Not all men were implacably opposed to the admission of women to the professions. John Stuart Mill argued from an economic perspective. In his seminal essay written in 1869, *The Subjection of Women*, he cited the law of supply and demand. He believed that women should not be forbidden from doing whatever they wanted to do and should not be prevented from entering the professions. If they were unable to compete with men, the market would select men rather than women and if they were better than men then the market place would employ them and permit them to thrive in the public sphere. If, he argued, they were naturally better at the private sphere activities, then there was no need to pass laws to keep them in the home as they would gravitate there naturally.[10]

Mary Daly tells us that marriage was the desired outcome for the majority of the prosperous middle and upper class Irish women of the nineteenth century, and that, once married, they very consciously neither contributed to family income nor to household chores. The woman of leisure devoting herself to accomplishments and to being a full time home-manager became the ideal. She suggests that the income earning wife was probably only acceptable among the lower reaches of the working classes and among farm labourers.[11]

Although middle-class urban women were not as directly impacted by the Famine as working class rural women were, the Famine (1845–49) influenced all sectors of Irish society. The marriage rate declined and women became conscious of their need to have an independent means of livelihood if they should fail to secure a husband. After the Famine, historians suggest that economic circumstances conspired to make Ireland an increasingly male-dominated society with a dramatic decline in the marriage rate. The bargaining position for women in both the employment and marriage markets was very poor. Education and emigration were the two strategies adopted by Irish women in the late 1800s and early 1900s in their search to acquire an income. Middle-class women saw entry into the professions as a possible option for them if they were not successful in entering the profession of marriage and did not wish to emigrate.[12]

Women's Suffrage and Equality – The Influence of the Armed Struggle

By the early 1900s, the Irish women's movement was becoming established and a number of (mainly Protestant) Irish women were involved in the movement and in the pursuit of female suffrage and equality, including equal rights to access the professions. As Europe became embroiled in the First World War, the European women's movements became diverted from the struggle for suffrage and equality towards the debate about militarism and pacifism. Many women's groups sought an end to the bloody carnage and supported pacifism. Other women concentrated on the work of supporting 'our brave boys at the front'. For example, the Irish Women's Suffrage and Local Government Association postponed its suffrage work and got engaged in tasks such as making bandages for the wounded horses (yes, horses!) who were part of the war effort in France.[13] For others, this was a distraction from the principal objectives of suffrage and equality for women. In Ireland, women were faced with the additional dilemma of whether, in resisting the horrible loss of life on the European front, they must also resist the growing nationalism in Ireland if it involved the use of violence against the British oppressors. Thomas MacDonagh addressed a meeting of Irish suffragists and outlined his very anomalous position of being an advocate of peace in Europe, but supporting the use of force against the British in achieving Irish freedom.[14] Louie Bennett and Hanna Sheehy Skeffington differed on the issue of justifiable armed struggle and issues surrounding nationality, such as the campaign in 1918 to reject the Conscription Act and moves in 1919 to seek international women's support to:

> ...regain our birthright, the right to meet and work with other Nations on an equal plane ...[we seek your support] for Ireland in her legitimate struggle for rights of self-determination.[15]

The contribution of women to the struggle for independence and the debate surrounding pacifism added to the strained relations between the 'separatist nationalists' and the suffrage groups (who were willing to seek suffrage and equality from an English parliament). Focus on nationalism diluted some of the energy which had been expended on suffrage, equal rights to education and entry into the professions for women. Hanna Sheehy Skeffington wrote of the *Irish Citizen*:

> There can be no woman's paper without a woman's movement, without earnest and serious-minded women readers and thinkers – and these have dwindled perceptibly of late ... the women's movement merged into the national movement temporarily, at least, and women became patriots rather than feminists, and heroes' wives or widows rather than human beings, so now in Ireland, the national struggle overshadows all else.[16]

So, at the time of the opening up of the professions to women in Ireland in 1919, there was a small but articulate women's movement, largely led by Protestant women who were unionist in their politics. The women's movement was somewhat fragmented by the absorption of the energy of many of the Catholic women into the struggle for independence. By 1919, the professions that women sought to enter had been well established, and it is pertinent for us to understand how they developed.

The Development of the Modern Professions

The period of the industrial revolution in the late eighteenth and early nineteenth centuries and the expansion of agricultural business gave rise to significant opportunities for the middle-classes (i.e. middle-class men) to earn money and to apply their talents in new and entrepreneurial ways. This resulted in greater societal value being placed on money and the earning of money. There were extraordinary opportunities for young men of talent, energy and shrewdness. It was no longer assumed that a son would automatically follow in his father's and grandfather's trade.[17] This growth of entrepreneurial industrial and commercial activities led to the need for concomitant professional advice from architects, lawyers, engineers and accountants. This fuelled the growth of the professions. Women were specifically excluded as the professions developed and this exclusion inflamed the growing discontent among the middle-class women who were not happy with their role in this period of enormous societal change. Roberts and Coutts suggested that occupations such as accountancy were "… involved in a continual process of struggle to maintain and consolidate their privileged position in a capitalist society", and that the feminization of the professions was "… perceived as a possible threat to patriarchal power structures".[18]

Although the industrial revolution was not as pervasive in Ireland as it was elsewhere in Europe, there were considerable opportunities for the growth of a middle-class business and professional class. The opportunities for men were not matched by equal opportunities for women and their role was still seen as the exercise of their influence in the domestic sphere on their husbands and children. Women were not permitted to join the professions and were dissuaded from engaging in business. They were encouraged into the public sphere in a very limited way. In the difficult industrial relations and social situations that were emerging in the 1830s and 1840s, women became important in the exercise of their influence and their caring skills in mitigating the worst effects of the industrialised society by engaging in philanthropic activities.

As the professions developed, their boundaries were protected by exclusivity of access. Entry to professions was limited by criteria, some stipulated and some understood, which included education, status and cultural tradition. Gender was a specific and clearly articulated entry restriction. This was not peculiar to Ireland and throughout Europe the need to preserve exclusivity contributed to restrictions on women entering professions.[19] If they were ever to succeed in entering the professions, women would first have to gain access to the education available to men and then secure the removal of the legal and bye-law prohibitions against women contained in many of the Charters of the Professional Bodies. The Institutes of Chartered Accountants had such specific prohibitions against the acceptance of women student or full members.

Prohibitions against women's entry to the professions were powerful deterrents and more robust than customary gendered practice in other fields of endeavour. In 1903, in Britain, Gray's Inn made a mistake and admitted Bertha Cave to its Honourable Society. But it subsequently refused to call her to the Bar, simply because she was a woman.

The original professions of the law, medicine and the Church had clearly defined entry routes – which excluded women. At the end of the nineteenth century, these professions and the newer professions which included engineering, architecture and accountancy, began to develop access routes which were tightly controlled. In Ireland (as in England, Scotland and Wales) the professional men sought Royal Charters to restrict entry and to establish the parameters of professional conduct. The professionalization project was fundamentally gendered and its success was not just a matter of creating an elite corps to which access was restricted, but also of establishing and maintaining a masculine identity for the professional accountant.[20]

The professions became very powerful and entry and control was strictly managed in order to protect their status. Elliott described the professionalization process as a dynamic process operating at three levels:

- First, the level of social change: the development of occupational professions is a key element in this process of managing specialisation during periods of rapid commercial and industrial development.
- Second, the level of occupational organisation: where society sets out the variety of ways in which a set of workers aspire to achieve professional status.
- Third, at the level of the individual life-cycle: focusing on the way in which individuals become practising members of a particular profession.[21]

A study of the census records dating from 1870 to 1930 reveals that, as part of the professionalization project, the professional accountant came to be constituted as neither a bookkeeper nor a clerk. This study categorised the professionalization project as one that was fundamentally gendered, the success of which necessitated creating and maintaining a masculine identity for the 'professional accountant'. Women were specifically excluded by the constitutions of all the early "qualifying societies" and, whilst a few women did practice accountancy, applications from them for membership of the professional bodies were "immediately rejected".[22]

The professionalization project did not just apply to the newer professions that developed to support the industrial revolution. As an example of the professionalization of the older professions, in 1858, following the passage of the Medical Act, medicine in Britain adopted all the characteristics of a profession. The medical profession (including the practitioners in Ireland) vehemently resisted escalating demands from women to be admitted to medicine.[23]

Some professions were available to women. However, they did not have to comply with the criteria for classification as a profession and quickly became female dominated and stereotyped and their role classified as 'women's work'. These professions included teaching, nursing, social work and librarianship. There was a fear that allowing women to enter third level education and to study for, *inter alia*, professional degrees would damage the professions and the women themselves. It was suggested that they would lose their femininity and even damage their health with too much study – even if they were able to pass the examinations. Society would suffer if women did not concentrate their efforts on the private sphere, on their marriages, homes and children.[24] In an editorial in August 1913, the *Irish Citizen* referred to the purported reasons against allowing women into the professions:

> *No one denies that a woman is capable of taking a gold medal in Logics or passing an LLD except that we are being constantly told that, in practical subjects, our brains and judgements are not to be trusted; we would be sure to make mistakes; nature has set certain traps for us.*

Arguments were advanced by doctors to establish categorically that higher education would damage women's health. Women's brains were too small to hold the required knowledge, their reproductive organs would atrophy and too much education would make them unable and unwilling to participate in marital and maternal roles.[25]

In the development of newer professions, the Institute of Chartered Accountants offers a useful exemplar. The first evidence of a firm of public accountants in Dublin was in 1761. Wilson's Dublin Directory, which listed several thousand merchants and traders, listed Thomas Hogan, carrying on business as merchant and accomptant (sic.) at 46 South King Street, Stephen's Green Dublin. Thom's Directory which superseded Wilson's Directory showed a steady growth of public accountants and in 1856 the first public accounting partnership was listed under the name Curry and Shields. In 1858, W. G. Craig left the Bank of Ireland where he had been employed and the second Irish accountancy partnership was announced – this was the beginning of the firm which became known as Craig Gardner & Co and subsequently PricewaterhouseCooper. By 1861 the list had increased to 43 and the name of Joseph H. Woodworth appears. Woodworth was, in 1888, to be one of the signatories to the Royal Charter and his grand-daughter was to be the first woman member of the Institute of Chartered Accountants in Ireland in 1925. In 1876, Stokes Bros. & Pim (subsequently to become Stokes Kennedy, Crowley and then KPMG) came into existence.[26] Unlike Craig Gardner & Co., this was a Protestant firm and its partners and articled clerks (with a few exceptions) were Protestant.[27]

In 1888, the leading 13 Dublin accountants joined with 12 accountants from Belfast and six from Cork recognising the need to professionalise their activities and petitioned for a Royal Charter from the British Crown. At this stage, there were no women public accountants.[28] The Royal Charter (see below) made provision for only male associates and fellows. By 1909, there was still no reference to female members and the Council minutes make no reference to any application by females for membership.

The Irish Institute survived the troubled days in Ireland between 1913 and 1938.[29] In the main, the members of the Institute of Chartered Accountants supported the Union with Britain and the Irish Institute preceded the Institutes in England Wales, and Scotland in deeming military service in the 1914–18 War as part of the articles of clerkship. Of course, some of the early members were nationalist – the most famous being Michael Collins who was an articled clerk in Craig, Gardner and Co.[30] Arthur Griffith was scathing in his condemnation of the Institute's pro-British leanings, although he made no suggestion that Irish women should be members or should even aspire to equality of treatment by the Institute, in spite of the assurance of the 1916 Proclamation, which assured that:

> The Republic guarantees religious and civil liberty, equal rights and equal opportunities to all its citizens, and declares its resolve to pursue the happiness and prosperity of the whole nation and all of its parts, cherishing all of the children of the nation equally …

This led to the subsequent 1922 Constitution (Article 3):

> Every person, without distinction of sex, domiciled in the area of the jurisdiction of the Irish Free State (Saorstát Éireann) at the time of the coming into operation of this Constitution, who was born in Ireland or either of whose parents was born in Ireland or who has been ordinarily resident in the area of the jurisdiction of the Irish Free State for not less than seven years, is a citizen of the Irish Free State and shall, within the limits of the Jurisdiction of the Irish Free State enjoy the privileges and be subject to the obligations of such citizenship.

THE ROUTE TAKEN BY WOMEN TO JOIN THE PROFESSIONS

Education

In spite of the strong resistance of society and the professions themselves, women, albeit in small numbers, struggled to gain the place in the professions promised to them by the Proclamation and the first Constitution. This was a common struggle internationally. In the 19th and early 20th centuries, women were excluded from the holding of public office, the universal franchise and standing for parliament. Additionally, there were restrictions on the holding of property and on involvement in trade, commerce and the professions. The aims of the early moderate feminists were primarily economic in character, involving the right to economic independence, the right for married women to control their own property and the admission of unmarried women to the professions, along with equal access to education for women.

In Europe in general, the struggle for female suffrage led to similar demands: the opening of the professions to unmarried women and property rights and other rights for married women. Everything came back to the right to equal education. If women were not admitted to the degree programmes in medicine, law and commerce, they had no chance of securing a place in any profession. Women recognised that their first step was through education.

Considerable work had gone into preparing the ground for these early professional women. Isabella Tod and others had ensured that the Intermediate Education Act (1878) allowed girls to present themselves for competitive public examinations on the same terms as boys. In 1873, she appealed for support for Gladstone's (unsuccessful) Bill for the Extension of University Education in Ireland:

> *We must draw the attention of the government and the legislature to the facts of the case, and claim from them that, in arranging for the higher education of one half of the nation, they shall not shut out the other half from its advantages.*[31]

Equal access for women to examination was secured under the terms of the University Education Act (1879). Although women could now present themselves for the examinations of the Royal University of Ireland, there was no provision for educational facilities for women in the universities.[32] Protestant girls could study in private colleges such as Victoria College in Belfast and Alexandra College in Dublin. In order to facilitate Catholic women, the Dominican convent in Eccles Street provided university classes in 1882 and they were followed by the Loreto order in Dublin and the Ursulines in Cork.[33]

In 1896 a memorial, signed by a group of distinguished peers of the realm and professional men and women academics and teachers was submitted to the Irish Chief Secretary, A. J. Balfour, and subsequently to the Robertson Commission (1903), supporting the financial funding of women in Irish universities, to give upper and middle-class women the educational advantages to allow them entry to the professions.

The access of Irish women to University education to prepare them for the professions was heavily influenced by the experience in England. Women's colleges were opened from the mid-1800s and by 1895 most[34] of the British universities opened their degrees to women. In Ireland, as mentioned above, women could present themselves for examination but could not attend the lectures and, in his letter dated 9 October 1873, the Secretary of the Queen's Institute, A. B. Corlett, appealed to the Board and Provost of Trinity College for the inclusion of women as full students and referred to the inadequacy of the examination only system in facilitating the progression of graduates to the professions.

Ten years later, Queen's College Belfast admitted women to their degree programmes and Queen's College, Cork admitted women in 1885. Galway followed in 1888. Trinity did not admit women until 1904. The majority of these early women graduates were Protestant and, due to the Catholic Church's initial opposition to the establishment of schools to prepare Catholic girls for examination, the Catholic women who wished to prepare themselves for university examination either had to attend Protestant institutions such as Alexandra College or prepare themselves privately. Margaret Downes, in 1888,[35] published the grievances of the Catholic women students who wished to gain access to the professions on an equal footing with men.

It was not until the Universities Act 1908 that women were admitted to all degrees and offices in the Universities of Queens University and the National University of Ireland.

However, access to university education did not guarantee access to the professions. Very few women graduates managed to enter the professions and their fight to enter university on an equal footing with men was only the beginning of the struggle for equality in the professions. There was some growth of employment opportunities for women in a number of the professions during the First World War, as the men left to serve in the forces, but it declined as they returned after the war. An anti-feminist, counter attack began which soon had professional women on the defensive, applying pressure on women who had been professionally employed during the war years to surrender their jobs to the 'more deserving' officers returning from the front.[36] By the end of the 1920s there was general societal acceptance that women could not marry and have children and pursue a career at the same time and this sentiment was copper-fastened by the marriage bars which remained in place until 1973.

WOMEN ENTER THE PROFESSIONS

The medical profession

The Irish medical profession was ahead of accountancy in admitting women. The Medical Act 1858 had formalised the exclusion of women from the scientific education of doctors and hence their registration as practitioners, but the Royal College of Physicians of Ireland voted to open its examinations to women in 1876, although it was not until the 1890s that the first female members of the medical profession qualified and worked in Ireland. During the 1890s, 35 women qualified as medical practitioners in Irish medical schools. All were qualified in medicine, surgery and midwifery and, although most of them were Irish, only fifteen of these 35 graduates were practising medicine in Ireland by 1900. The rest were working in England or, in many cases, as medical missionaries. By 1911, the Medical Directory showed that the number had increased to 42.

Even though medical education was expensive, the cost was not thought to be the factor that deterred families from encouraging their daughters to enter the profession. Families were, for example, very willing to provide the large dowries that were required for Catholic girls entering the convent. It was, rather, the strong societal expectation that women should remain in the domestic sphere which made it difficult for them to access professional careers. Indeed, sometimes the best opportunity for Catholic women was by taking the veil and then accessing the professions as nuns. However, most of the early doctors in Ireland were Protestant and, in fact, the first doctors qualifying as practitioners, in particular women like Katharine Maguire, Amelia Grogan and Kathleen Lynn,[37] were daughters of Church of Ireland rectors.

The legal profession

The legal profession was as tardy as accountancy in admitting women. Women seeking to enter the legal profession as solicitors and barristers met a wall of resistance from the male-dominated legal profession. *The Irish Citizen*, in April 1914, reported that the Lord Chancellor was hopeful about the introduction of a Bill authorising women to be solicitors and about the possibility of having it passed by the end of that session. Two Bills were referred to, but that proposed by Viscount Wolman was preferred by the editor, since it permitted women to be barristers as well as solicitors. Although Kathleen Clarke acted as a 'judge' in the Sinn Féin courts set up under the aegis of the first Dáil after the 1918 election, it was not until the introduction of the 1919 Sex Disqualification Act that women were formally permitted to enter the legal profession. The basic purpose of that Act was, as stated in its long title, "... to amend the Law with respect to disqualification on account of sex", which it achieved in four short sections and one Schedule. Its broad aim was achieved by Section 1, which stated that:

> *A person shall not be disqualified by sex or marriage from the exercise of any public function, or from being appointed to or holding any civil or judicial office or post, or from entering or assuming or carrying on any civil profession or vocation, or for admission to any*

incorporated society (whether incorporated by Royal Charter or otherwise), and a person shall not be exempted by sex or marriage from the liability to serve as a juror.

Section 1 was very sweeping and broad, applying to all professions. Section 2 allowed for the admission of women specifically as solicitors, provided they had served three years and possessed a University degree. Section 3 prohibited the exclusion of women from Universities and Section 4 ruled that any royal charters (including that of the Institute of Chartered Accountants), orders in council or statutory provisions in contravention with this law were to cease to have effect. The first woman to become a solicitor, Carrie Morrison, did not qualify until 1923.

The accountancy profession

In the accountancy profession, the first woman to have an accountancy post is thought to be Barbara Verschoyle, who was the agent for the Fitzwilliam estate from the 1780s until 1827. However, this was long before the Royal Charter established the profession of Chartered Accountancy in 1888.

Women in the early decades of the twentieth century worked in large numbers in white collar clerical jobs, including book-keeping. There were just over 2,000 women engaged in clerical occupations in 1891 and this had increased to 9,747 by 1911.[38] Also, women had been involved in book-keeping in family businesses for much longer. Thomas Russell, of the United Irishmen, noted in his diary in 1793 that women, in merchants' houses, kept the accounts as well as men. Their numbers were small, but it is possible that an exposure to a book-keeping job might have given intelligent women a taste for advancement to the accountancy profession.

In 1901 the minutes of the Council of the Institute of Chartered Accountants in Ireland show that Edward Kevans, an accountant in practice, whose son Patrick had served with him as an articled clerk from 1889, qualifying in 1897, applied for his daughter Cecily to be admitted as a student member. In this pre-Independence and pre-First World War 1 environment in Dublin it is possible to imagine the scene from the photographic records of the Institute. The newly formed profession comprised a solid body of men, all in austere suits and white shirts with their precisely sculpted goatees and pince-nez glasses jammed uncompromisingly against gloomy eyes gazing suspiciously at copperplate accounts prepared by their young articled clerks. They were creating a new profession – a new image – a new status. They were not mere clerks or book-keepers. They were professionals, like doctors, lawyers and clerics. They were conservative, prudent, circumspect, careful and entirely male. In their lives, the role of women was as wife and mother. Those Council members must have had grave reservations about an application from a lady, but they decided to check it out with London. The Institute in Dublin consulted the Institute of Chartered Accountants in England and Wales (which also forbade lady students or members) to seek advice about this suggestion that a lady should be admitted. There was stiff opposition from London to the idea and they strongly objected to such a move.[39] Faced with such formidable opposition, Kevans withdrew his application and his daughter was not permitted to join him and her brother in his practice.[40]

At the time, there were women CPAs in the United States of America. Christine Ross had begun practising accountancy in 1889, working for Manning's Yacht Agency. In practice, her clients included women's organisations, wealthy women and the fashion industry. She was the first woman to sit for the New York State CPA exam in 1898, scoring second of her group. Eighteen months elapsed while her certificate was delayed by state regents on account of her gender. But she had completed the requirements and became the first woman CPA in the United States, receiving certificate no. 143 on Dec. 21, 1899. Reports of the experience of those early women accountants in the USA were discouraging. A report in a professional journal, relating to ladies in the profession said:

> When a member of an accounting staff is engaged, it is understood that he is to hold himself in readiness to serve whenever and wherever called upon to do so. In the wide variety of modern accounting practice a staff member may be required to go from one end of the country to another, in company with groups of staff members, working at high pressure and under living conditions not suitable

for what might be termed post-graduate co-education. Then, again, there are many assignments to which staff members are sent, involving working all night long in places of difficulty and inconvenience. For example an audit of a bank must be performed between hours of closing and opening. Large numbers of men are sent to work, but any attempt at heterogeneous personnel would hamper progress and lead to infinite embarrassment.[41]

One wonders what exactly he had in mind. In all my years of auditing banks and other business enterprises, both in town and out of town, both during the hours of daylight and darkness, I completely missed out on the experience of being sent off with a large number of men to engage in progress-impeding, embarrassing activities of a co-educational nature. (I am left with a vague sense of disappointment.)

This 19th Century concern for the morals of both the men and women reflects the same concern expressed when women tried to gain access to lectures and to halls of residence in the Universities. Indeed, ladies would not even be served with a pot of tea in most hotels, unless accompanied by a gentleman.

Finally, In 1919, following the passing of the Sex Disqualification (Removal) Act, the minutes of the Irish Institute of Chartered Accountants thirty-first annual meeting, held at its offices in 39 Fleet Street, Dublin show that the President, Mr. Stewart Blacker Quinn referred to the resolution to be considered by the meeting:

As the matter stands, we have been legally advised that under the terms of our Charter, we have no power to admit ladies to membership and, therefore, it will be necessary for the Institute to obtain powers for this object. We have already received applications for the admission of ladies and, having regard to the great position ladies have now won for themselves, a number of members of the Council feel that the Institute of Chartered Accountants should progress with the times and that ladies should be admitted to membership. As the admission of ladies to the Institute would involve Parliamentary sanction, I have been bold enough to suggest to the Council that the Institute, in promoting a Bill in Parliament empowering the admission of women as members, should also include in the Bill

*comprehensive proposals for the setting up of a register of all prac-
tising accountants in Ireland and a scheme for the registration and
future control of our profession.*

Following some debate a resolution to permit the admission of
women to the Institute was passed by "a large majority". The wording
of the resolution made it very clear that women were to be admitted
on exactly the same terms and conditions as men and subject to the
same rights and duties:

> *That women shall be allowed to qualify for membership of the Insti-
> tute of Chartered Accountants in Ireland and that on duly qualify-
> ing they shall be eligible for admission to the rights, privileges and
> benefits of membership of the said Institute....*

It was not until 1925 that the first woman was admitted to full
membership of the Institute, having been admitted as a student
member in 1920. She was Eileen Woodworth, whose grandfather was
one of the original signatories to the Charter. She married Norman
McAllister in 1930 and practised in Rangoon with a break of one
year in 1932. She continued to practise during the war years and
died in Madras in July 1942. She must have been a considerable
feminist of her time to qualify as the only woman among almost
200 chartered accountants and to continue in practice subsequent to
her marriage. Kathleen O'Neill was the second woman. She was the
daughter of John O'Neill, managing director of John O'Neill Ltd, a
motor company and of Beleek Pottery Ltd. He was a founder member of the Dublin Industrial Development Association and a promi-
nent member of several government financial committees. Although
he had a large family, he sent his daughter to university where she
graduated with a commerce degree. She was accepted into articles
with Kean & Co and qualified in 1926. She subsequently entered the
Dominican Convent, Sion Hill having completed a H.Dip. in Education and became the college bursar in St. Mary's Training College in
Belfast. They were followed by a trickle of women which included
Emma Bodkin, a daughter of Judge Bodkin and sister of Thomas
Bodkin, until, by 1973 (when the marriage bar was raised under a
European Directive) the trickle had increased to a grand pool of 19
lady members in Ireland (north and south).[42]

MARRIAGE AND HAVING A PROFESSIONAL CAREER

Many of the early historical accounts of women entering the professions assumed that entry was for single women who eschewed married life and the possibility of motherhood. The *Irish Citizen,* in 1914, carried a report of a decision by Dublin County Council that women medical officers should retire on marriage. (The same paper, coincidentally, noted that an important new microbial scientific principle had just been discovered by Madame Henry – a married medical woman.) By today's standards, the spectacle of a Board of city men deciding what duties outside the home well-qualified women may undertake would be entirely comic if it were not so unfair.

Following the First World War, the problem of the 'surplus women' was a factor in understanding the role of women. Jobs that had been filled by women whilst the men were at war had to be surrendered to the returning officers in 1918, as mentioned earlier. Women suffered the double whammy of having to concede their professional posts and of being forced to fill the alternative profession offered to them – that of wife and mother. However, husbands were hard to come by among the seriously depleted and disabled ranks of men returning from the war and the option of having a child out of wedlock was simply unthinkable. This state of affairs remained for Irish women until membership of the EU opened windows of equality in many fields of endeavour. Today, a person's marital status can play no part in deciding whether s/he is suitable for a position.

SLOW PROGRESS IN THE POST-INDEPENDENCE YEARS

In 1922, the first Constitution provided, *inter alia,* for equality, and it codified the aspiration of the 1916 Proclamation. By then, the formal exclusion of women from the professions had been lifted by the 1919 Sex Disqualification Act. Women could enter university and could apply to be admitted to the professions, provided they had the appropriate entry requirements. However, the numbers of women in the professions in 1922 was very small and, in the main, they were single and Protestant. The years of Irish independence that followed were not blossoming years for the opening out of professions, including the accountancy profession, to women. Although the introduction of the equality provision in the 1922 Constitution must have made women optimistic about the prospects for the future and, in particular, about equality of treatment and opportunity for men and women, there were several factors that militated against the implementation of such equality:

1. The position of the Roman Catholic Church (largely supported by the State) was that women should remain in the home and have families unrestricted by contraception. There was a uniquely Irish view that women should remain in the home after marriage and that Roman Catholic women should produce and rear large families. Protestant women were not influenced by this exhortation, but were subjected to the Victorian views of subjugation of personal ambitions in the interests of family and philanthropic service, and they were also subjected to the marriage bars.

2. The 1937 Constitution (Bunreacht na hÉireann) introduced specific reference to the special place of women in the home. The emphasis on equality which had been included in the Proclamation and in the 1922 Constitution was dropped.

3. Irish women had been included in decision-making and in affairs of State during and following the 1916 Rising. They would have been forgiven for assuming that they would continue to be involved at every level of society once the independent government had broken free of the shackles of the colonial power. However, in spite of their contribution to the liberation struggle, and in spite of the legal provision for equality contained in the 1922 Constitution, they soon learned that the mindset of men cannot be instantly changed. The 1936 Conditions of Employment Act empowered the government to introduce controls on women's employment (attempting to deal with the unemployment problem by replacing women workers with men),[43] marriage bars in the public service, non-compulsory jury service for women, differential salary scales for male and female teachers and the recognition of nationality only through the father. President Éamon de Valera, meeting a deputation of women who resisted these retrograde steps, said that he 'could not see how men and women could be equal'.[44]

Despite their legal right to enter the professions, the numbers of women actually taking up that right was, as indicated above, pitifully small and it was not until after our entry into the European Common Market (now the EU) that numbers began to approach equality. The few women who entered the professions were pioneers and Virginia Woolf's speech to a group of professional women on "Professions for Women" has resonance:

> *She is one of the race of the pioneers. She is among the ice-breakers, the window-smashers, the indomitable and irresistible armoured tanks who climbed the rough ground: went first; drew the enemy's fire and left a pathway for those who came after her. I never knew whether to be angry that such heroic pertinacity was called for, or glad that it had the chance of showing itself.*[45]

Many of the early Irish professional women emigrated and did not practise in Ireland. This indicates a sense of pessimism about staying in Ireland, particularly if they wanted to get married, have a family and continue with their professional career. Probably this overriding sense of pessimism that must have been experienced by the early Irish aspirants to equal entry into the professions with an equal opportunity to practise is best summed up in this comment by Dora Mellone: '... we know quite well that by slow degrees women have won admission to almost all the professions ... but we still have difficulty obtaining work and the under payment for the work, when obtained, is sufficiently serious'.[46]

THE 21ST CENTURY

The situation with regard to the equal admission of women to membership of the accountancy profession in the United States and in other Anglo-American influenced environments, including Ireland, had normalised by the beginning of the 21st Century. The number of women has gradually increased to the present time when the percentage of women admitted to membership of the Institute of Chartered Accountants in Ireland is now (2009) 54% and the total percentage of women members is 30%.

We have seen that women had a struggle to obtain access to the profession of accountancy, similar to the struggle to gain access to other professions. By the time of writing, this issue of equality of **access** has been resolved. However, the issue of equality of **opportunity to progress** to the upper reaches of the profession is far from resolution and remains a source of much concern to the members of the profession and, in particular, to the accountancy firms who stand to gain from the retention of bright and productive women. The statistics show a stark picture of the obstacles to progression. The 54% female student intake and yet 70% male membership of the Institute of Chartered Accountants might be explained if equal access to women had only opened up in recent years and if the total membership was heavily dominated by older members admitted when there were few women. However, nearly 70% of the total membership is younger than 45 years, so membership cannot be said to be skewed for this reason. The statistics show that women are being admitted to membership in equal numbers and have been since 1988,[47] but they are not staying in the profession in the same ratio as men. Additionally, in Ireland and internationally, they are not progressing to the top of the profession in proportion to their representation at admission. (See Table 1.1.)

Women in the US hold 13.2% of Big Four partnerships and in the UK, although more than 52% of all accountancy students are female, only 9% of the partners in the top 60 firms are female. Women in practice are not securing and holding the elite positions. In the Big

Table 1.1 Number and percentage of women partners in the Big Four Firms

Firm	Total no. of partners	Number of women partners	Percentage of women partners
KPMG	85	11	13%
PWC	90	19	21%
Ernst & Young	46	6	13%
Deloittes	45	7	15%
Total	266	43	16%

Four firms in Ireland, the numbers (and percentages) of women partners (disclosed to the author) at May 2008 were:

This problem is not unique to the accountancy profession. Women now outnumber men at entry level to the legal professions in Ireland. However, at the upper end of the legal professions, women have failed to break through, despite their increased entry levels since the 1970s and despite statutory support for equality. In the large legal practices, only one has a female managing partner and in only two do women make up more than 30% of the partners. Additionally, women tend to move jobs more frequently than men and are more likely to work as employed lawyers than their male counterparts.[48]

SUMMARY

It is clear that, in the 90 years since the opening up of the accountancy profession to women in Ireland, access is equally available to women and men, but progression to the top of the professional firms, to the elite position of partner, still presents difficulties for women.

There are significant barriers and obstacles that women have experienced in entering this all male preserve. Chapter 3 briefly reviews those obstacles. There has been considerable emphasis in the past on difficulties and barriers. However, although we cannot ignore the well-documented evidence of the sometimes gross, but often subtle obstacles, we mustn't allow it to overwhelm us. We must be cognisant of the history of exclusion and barriers, of course, but it would be more positive, if, instead of concentrating on the problems and difficulties of competing equally with men in the accountancy profession, we were to look at the experience of the women who have done it successfully, rather than bewailing the lot of those who have not. So Chapter 4 adopts a positive approach rather than a negative one and attempts to identify and harness the qualities of success rather than the obstacles to progression. But first, let us, in the next chapter, paint the backdrop to the barriers and obstacles.

REFERENCES

1. Gregory J. (1774), *A Father's Legacy to his Daughters*, Garland Publishing, New York.
2. Ibid. pp 6, 7.
3. Fordyce J. (1794), *Sermons to young Women*, Millar, Law and Cater, London, pp 1–24, 26, 213.
4. Gisborne T. (1798), *An Enquiry into the Duties of the Female Sex*, John Humphries, Philadelphia.
5. *Edinburgh Review* (1810), *Rights and Conditions of Women*, Edinburgh Review, 23 January.
6. Ellis S. (1845), *The Daughters of England*, Fortescue Press, London.
7. Gaskell E. (1967), *The Letters of Mrs Gaskell*, ed. Chapple J. A., and Pollard A., Harvard University Press, Cambridge, Mass.
8. Newton J. (1981), *Women's Time* in *Feminisms*, Warhol R. and Herndl D. (eds) (1997), Rutgers University Press, New Brunswick.
9. Tod I. M. (1874), On the Education of Girls of the Middle-Classes, in Luddy M. (ed.), 1996, *Women in Ireland, 1800–1918: A Documentary History*, Cork, pp 108–110.
10. Mill J. S. (1869), *The Subjection of Women*, cited in Evans R. J. (ed.) (1977), *The Feminists*, Croom Helm, London.
11. Daly M. (1981), *Women in the Irish Workforce from Pre-Industrial to Modern Times*, in Saothar 7.
12. Lee J. (1978), Women and the Church since the Famine, in MacCurtain M., and O'Corrain D. (eds) *Women in Irish Society: The Historical Dimension*, Dublin (1978).
13. See Rosemary Cullen-Owen's excellent *A Social History of Women in Ireland 1870–1970*, Gill & Macmillan, Dublin, for a clear analysis of these issues p. 13.
14. Reported in *The Irish Citizen*, 22 May 1915.
15. Women's International League for Peace and Freedom, Colorado, May 1919.
16. Hanna Sheehy-Skeffington, 1920, *The Irish Citizen*, November–December 1920.
17. Hobsbawn E. J. (1962), *The Age of Revolution 1789–1848*, New American Library, New York.
18. Roberts J and Coutts A. (1992), Feminization and Professionalization: A Review of an Emerging Literature on the Development of Accounting, *Accounting, Organizations and Society*, pp 379–395.
19. Simonton D. (1998), *A History of European Women's Work -1700 to Present*, Routledge, London.
20. Kirkham L. M. and Loft A. (1993), Gender and the Construction of the Professional Accountant, *Accounting, Organizations and Society*, 1993, pp 507–558.
21. Elliot P. (1972), *The Sociology of the Professions*, Macmillan Press, London.
22. Kirkham & Loft ibid.

23. Finn I. (2000), Women in the Medical Profession in Ireland, 1876–1919, in Whelan B. (ed.), *Women and Paid Work in Ireland, 1500–1930,* Four Courts Press, Dublin.

24. See Burstyn J., 'Education and Sex: The Medical Case against Higher Education for Women in England, 1870–1900' in *Proceedings of the American Philosophical Society,* Vol. 117, 1973 pp 79–89.

25. See Phyllis Stock (1978), *Better than Rubies: A History of Women's Education,* London: 1978.

26. Robinson H. (1983), *History of Accountants in Ireland,* The Institute of Chartered Accountants in Ireland, Dublin.

27. In 1973, there was a considerable stir in Dublin when this Protestant firm merged with Kennedy Crowley & Co, a Roman Catholic firm which had been established in 1880.

28. During this period, Ireland suffered many financial disasters, not least in the banking sector. The most renowned was the demise, in 1885, of the Munster Bank – later to re-emerge from the ashes as the Munster and Leinster Bank. Robinson (1983) says of the late 1800s:

    > *Wild speculation, dishonesty, failures, were perhaps inevitable children of the Industrial Revolution, but just as inevitable was the creation of the profession of accountancy as a safeguard to protect the public against these evils. Ireland was not predominant, either as regards speculations or frauds, but was engulfed by the wave that passed over these islands last century and produced its quota of accountants in an attempt to master it. p.36*

29. Of all Irish bodies, only the Institute of Chartered Accountants and the Irish Rugby Football Association survived the political turmoil of World War I, the Rebellion and the establishment of the Free State undivided as between the Republic and the North of Ireland.

30. Robinson, ibid.

31. Tod I., ibid.

32. Breathneach E. (1987), Charting New Waters: Women's Experience in Higher Education, 1879–1908, in Cullen M. (ed.), *Girls Don't Do Honours: Irishwomen in Education in the Nineteenth and Twentieth Centuries,* Dublin, pp 55–76.

33. Cullen M. and Luddy M. (eds), (1995), *Women, Power and Consciousness in 19th Century Ireland,* Dublin.

34. Oxford did not award full degrees to women on the same terms as men until 1919 and Cambridge did not do so until 1921.

35. Downes M. (1888), The Case of the Catholic Lady Students of the Royal University Stated, cited in Raferty and Parkes (2007), *Female Education in Ireland 1700–1900,* Irish Academic Press, Dublin.

36. See, for a discussion of the position of single women following World War I, Nicholson V. (2008), *Singled Out,* Penguin Books, London.

37. Probably better known for her role in the 1916 uprising and contribution to the opening of St Ultan's Infant Hospital in 1919.

38. Luddy M. (2000), Women and Work in Nineteenth and Early Twentieth Century Ireland, in Whelan B. (ed.), *Women and Paid Work in Ireland 1500–1930,* Four Courts Press, Dublin.
39. Barker P. (1988), The True and Fair Sex, in Rowe D. (ed.), *The Irish Chartered Accountant: Centenary Essays,* Gill & Macmillan, Dublin.
40. Robinson H. (1983), *History of Accountants in Ireland,* The Institute of Chartered Accountants in Ireland, Dublin.
41. Richardson A. P. (1923), Editorial in the *Journal of Accountancy,* December 1923.
42. Barker P. (1988), The True and Fair Sex, in Rowe D. (ed.), *The Irish Chartered Accountant: Centenary Essays,* Gill & Macmillan, Dublin.
43. Owens R. (2005), *A Social History of Women in Ireland, 1870–1970,* Gill & Macmillan, Dublin.
44. Irish Women Workers' Union, Executive Minutes, 5th September 1935.
45. Woolf V. (1931), Professions for Women, in Leaska M. (1977), *The Pargiters,* Public Library and Readex Books: New York.
46. Mellone D. (1914), Women and the Professions, *The Irish Citizen,* 18/4/1914.
47. Barker P. (1988), The True and Fair Sex, in Rowe D. (ed.), *The Irish Chartered Accountant: Centenary Essays,* Gill & Macmillan, Dublin.
48. Bacik I., Costello C. and E. Drew (2003), *Gender Injustice,* Trinity College Dublin Law School, Dublin.

3

♦

BARRIERS AND OBSTACLES
TO PROGRESSION

Specific Gender-Based Obstacles?

By 1973, when Ireland's membership of the EU dictated the removal of the marriage bar, the number of women who had qualified as Chartered Accountants in Ireland was 19. Although numbers entering the profession have increased to a broadly 50:50 ratio by 2009, this ratio has not fed through to the top of the profession and women are not being appointed as partners of the Big Four firms in anything like that ratio. Additionally, more women 'quit' the partnership track than men. There are two forces at play here. Firstly, there are obstacles that women experience that are not experienced by men. Secondly, women themselves make different choices to men and they choose to 'quit' or 'flee' in greater numbers than men. This results in a loss of the diverse qualities that many women can offer. This loss of skills and competencies, which are expensive to acquire and develop, is a worrying feature for the profession. The firms are only fully harnessing half of the available intellectual capital pool. Additionally, if women have skills and competencies that men do not display, it means that the firms, in failing to retain their diverse and unique skills, lose that magic mixture of talents that give an organisation a competitive edge in today's difficult economic environment. What are these specific obstacles that women face and why are they quitting the partnership track? Let us explore these two issues:

What are the Specific Obstacles that Women Face?

There have been several attempts to explain why women did not flood into the professions once the gender barrier was raised in 1919. Of course, the marriage bar and other legal and societal barriers played a significant part, and analysis suggests that men shifted their strategy from exclusion to a strategy of separation.[1] It has been mooted that women's work was separated from men's work and was often valued less in terms of remuneration and status. For example, as women entered the teaching profession in larger numbers, the status and remuneration surrounding that profession declined. Conversely, we can observe that, as more men enter the nursing profession, its status and remuneration increase. There is some evidence that women, in the accountancy profession, tend to cluster in areas which require technical rather than problem-solving expertise and areas that are office-based rather than requiring significant business travel. However, they do not appear to have a lower status or significantly lower pay based on obvious gender discrimination.[2] So the separation theory does not seem to provide an explanation in this case.

Getting to the top of the accountancy profession and making it to partnership in a Big Four firm is a pathway strewn with difficulties and obstacles. There are obstacles that are not gender specific, such as for example:

- failure to display the intellectual and technical abilities that are required;
- not having the required interpersonal skills;
- inability to rise to the increasing pressure to retain existing and attract new clients;
- aversion to the difficulties arising from the post-Enron regulatory and supervisory environment and to the increasing risk.

The Octet of Obstacles

However, there are additional difficulties for women which are evident when the partnership statistics are broken down by gender. These may be considered under the following eight headings:

1. Difficulties in 'invading' an occupied space
2. Self-confidence
3. Leadership style
4. Adoption of male characteristics
5. Lack of mentoring
6. Discomfort with networking
7. Excessive working hours
8. Managing life/work balance

Difficulties in 'invading' an occupied space

The barriers for women accountants seem to have been more subtle
and complex than straightforward gender discrimination. Women
entered a space that had been designed by men, for men and to
serve male clients. After 1919, men did not prevent women from
entering, but they did little to encourage the invasion. Neither did
they take positive steps to make a space to allow the 'invaders' to
enter in sufficient numbers for them to have a critical mass which
would allow them to define their part of the space for themselves.
Indeed, the male incumbents probably saw no reason to do so
and are likely to have described themselves as being completely
fair and equitable, treating male and female trainees and professionals 'absolutely equally'. The training in Articles of Clerkship
and, subsequently, Training Contracts, was gender neutral, but
women were implicitly expected to fit into the model that had
already been established and tested. Women themselves probably
did not have the language to articulate the differences in the skills
and competencies they brought to the table. They entered the
male space in relatively small numbers and survived by disguising
their differences and blending into the male skill set established
by their predecessors.[3]

   In contrast, other areas of business, such as for example the
beauty industry, the specialist food industry, soft toys and the
child-care sector, have been developed by women entrepreneurs
who saw an economic opening for them to work mainly with
other women and to provide a service or product to women.
This exploitation by women of women-specific market business opportunities made it easier for women to define the work

place and work practices to suit themselves.[4] There are, of course, problems associated with having a workplace defined and populated entirely by women. This does not achieve diversity either. However, it was more difficult for women to enter the already established male environment of the accountancy profession than to engage professionally in an area constructed and defined by women for women and populated largely by women workers and clients. This difficulty presented an obstacle to women accountants not experienced by their male counterparts. (As an aside, we can note that, in more recent times, there are more women clients for the accountancy profession. However, there is no evidence that women clients seek out women professional accountants or indeed that women accountants seek out women clients or women staff and colleagues.)

Self-confidence

To succeed in achieving elite positions, there is no gender difference in the expectation that a candidate for partnership should be self-confident and have high self-esteem. Having a strong sense of belief in one's own ability is a valuable asset in any leadership role.[5] However, women often do not have the self-confidence of their male counterparts. They understand the necessity to display self-confidence, even if they do not feel it.[6] Women have shown a unique tendency to keep quiet about their successes, assuming that others will notice them without being prompted. They also have a tendency to take personal blame for their failures, confessing them loudly and widely. Often women believe that their successes were controlled by luck or by powerful others, whereas men are more likely to believe that luck was important, but that their success was due to their talent, hard work, tenacity and willingness to take advantage of opportunities offered. Clearly, such a simplistic distinction does not apply to *all* men and *all* women, but even if this dichotomy is not applicable in all cases, it is generally applicable and it is clear how this difference in self-confidence between men and women can be a barrier to many women who present themselves for assessment within a male model.

Leadership style

It is now widely accepted that there is a distinctive management style that women can bring to a management team. It has been described as a *transformational* style as opposed to the *transactional* style of management that men are more likely to use.[7] Women are associated with a more sensitive, inclusive and collaborative style of management, and women's 'soft skills' are now cited as essential for successful change management and team building.[8]

We know that women possess the necessary educational qualifications and skills for management and professional positions. Indeed, women managers are likely to possess higher qualifications than their male counterparts. However, women's unique skills are often not recognised or valued and, in male-dominated organisations, women perceive their feminine skills as less valuable and feel the need to enact gender roles that conform to men's preferences, thereby reinforcing male dominance.[9] Some women are comfortable in adopting male characteristics in their business life, but many are not. They find that the incongruence between their natural inclinations and the role they are expected to adopt creates a dissonance that is stressful and often leads to such high levels of stress that their own psychological well-being begins to suffer.[10] So, although women are not being discriminated against or excluded by male gate-keepers, they are quitting because of this incongruence. This, of course, results in a predominance of characteristic masculine behaviour being displayed both by men and the surviving women at top management level, although not necessarily at lower and middle management. This suggests that the elite women are likely to feel comfortable at top level if they either have a transactional management style or are comfortable about adopting such characteristics. The cognitive dissonance and stress experienced by many women between their natural management style and the style that is expected of them will be a barrier for them in progressing to top management.

Adopting male characteristics/behaviours

The barriers addressed so far:

1. Being invaders in a male space
2. Lacking a high sense of self-confidence and
3. Possessing skills and competencies that are under-valued

all contain another difficulty that is worthy of separate consideration. There is an assumption that women will overcome these difficulties if only they adopt male characteristics and compete with the men on the same terms. If they adopt a male model, and become honorary men, they would blend in rather than stand out, and compete on the terms already established by men and understood by them. This is not a new phenomenon and Simone de Beauvoir, born in 1908, signalled the necessity for a woman who wants to succeed in business to act like a man.[11] Women have, historically, provided instances where they, quite literally, masqueraded as men in order to enter and practise in professions such as medicine, the law and even the Papacy.

There has been a perception that women are not sufficiently logical or tough to succeed in leadership and that somehow their femininity is an impediment.[12] The implied solution to this problem was to become more like a man. Of course, this was rarely explicitly stated (except in satirical fiction such as *Pygmalion*) and sometimes only partially perceived. Pressure was often subtle, but was a cultural norm which everyone understood, even if there was little discourse around the issue. So, in spite of organisational acceptance of women and in spite of legal protection of equality, the deep-rooted structure of valued characteristics and behaviour is largely determined by male values.

However, to make things more complex, even though the pressure was on women to behave like men in business dealings, they were also expected to be feminine – even though the characteristics required were often contradictory. The conservatism of the profession would resist a cigar-puffing, pin-striped Amazon who 'kicked ass'. Some women were comfortable in accepting the challenge and managed to steer a safe course between the two dangers. On the one hand was the reef of over doing the modelling and becoming unduly aggressive and masculine; and, on the other hand, was the sandbank of clinging to their femininity at a cost of being branded as noisy feminists or constantly pre-menstrual. Others foundered and left the profession and yet others altered course and steered for a safer harbour, quitting the partnership track and selecting alternative accountancy careers in, for example, industry or academe, or as sole practitioners.

The key question is, of course, whether women should change their natural behaviour and behave like men or whether the women who succeed in making it to an elite position such as partner in a Big Four firm naturally display more masculine characteristics. Studies have shown that even though feminine characteristics are valued by the professional firms (particularly for change-management and human resource management),[13] the progression pathway is structured in a masculine way.[14] It would appear that women can compete with their male colleagues, especially if they are willing to adopt masculine characteristics at the top. This is a significant barrier to women who do not naturally display predominantly masculine characteristics and are not willing to adopt them.

Lack of mentoring

Studies show that one of the more serious barriers that women professionals experience is the failure of senior leaders to provide opportunities for visibility.[15] Compared with their male counterparts, women executives are less likely to have supportive mentoring to assist their progress.[16] Very few successful leaders, male or female, had female mentors. This has been attributed to:

- the scarcity of top women who could act as mentors:
- the possibility that women are not perceived as good mentors, because they are in a minority;
- stereotypes about the abilities of women and
- the possibility that women are unconscious of the need to mentor other women or unwilling to do so.[17]

It is very clear that progress to the top requires some support in getting past the gatekeepers. The top positions are controlled by those who have made it to the top themselves. They often seek young protégées to mentor whom they recognise as being like themselves.[18] Studies have shown the importance for women trying to rise in a male dominated culture of having a strong male mentor in the family and a strong professional female mentor.[19] The shortage of female mentors and their reluctance to act as 'woman-to-woman' supporters is a difficult obstacle for women to overcome.

Discomfort with networking

Although male and female leaders at the top of organisations are often in agreement when questioned about gender differentiation, there are two issues on which they disagree. Indeed male and female leaders at all levels of organisations disagree on these two issues. They are:

1. the need for women to be better than men to compete and
2. the importance of the informal network.

Men do not believe that women need to be better than them at any level to compete for promotion. Women do.[20]

Women are conscious of their lack of a network among colleagues, superiors and clients. They are also conscious of its importance if they want to progress. Men, on the other hand, accept building a network through school, university, golf, business, rugby, drinking and other contacts as such an intrinsic part of the way they do business, that they are almost oblivious of its operation. Studies show that the accountancy profession in Europe is characterised by aggressive entertaining and networking.[21] Time spent on the client can, among elite professionals, leak into private time and the response of women and men to this leeching of professional client time into time for social, domestic and private activities may be different. Male accountants seem more willing to spend time on the golf course, in the bar and in social activities with clients than women accountants.[22] Irish women accountants suffer from the lack of a female network and have referred to their exclusion from the entrenched male sports networks of golf, rugby and the GAA. Women do little to participate in this network or even to create networks around female activities, but they perceive their exclusion as a barrier that is placed by others, albeit unconsciously.

Excessive working hours

Time is a very valuable commodity to all of us today and there is much discussion in the literature of life/work balance. Time is the commodity that professional accountants sell and availability and willingness to spend effective time on the clients' problems as and when they arise is one of the factors that distinguish those at the top of the profession from those who never achieve elite status. The hours spent at work for a professional accountant on the partnership track are excessive by any standard. They would certainly total 60 hours per week and often exceed this. Additionally, candidates for partnership must be willing to be contacted by clients in the evenings, at the weekend and when they are on holiday. The inflexibility of the large professional offices in terms of constructing other models of time and availability to the client is one of the obstacles to progression for many women.[23] Many women are less willing to accept the hours of work needed to support the needs of clients around the clock than their male counterparts. Engagement in this level of client support requires relative freedom from domestic ties which is more likely to apply to men than women.

Managing life/work balance

Men and women all try to achieve life-work balance and endeavour to find time to spend with their families, friends and on outside interests as well as pursuing their high-powered careers. However, among elite business people, women are significantly more likely than men to report having made sacrifices by deferring or eschewing parenthood in order to devote themselves to the pursuit of their careers. Even the capacity to pay for childcare and domestic support is not sufficient to allow these women to fulfil their family aspirations, and so they postpone motherhood.[24] Women professionals believe that, unlike their male counterparts, it is not possible for women to 'have it all' i.e. a successful professional career and a family.[25]

Studies show a trend for both spouses* in a professional couple to be in careers but also a disproportionate allocation of the domestic work load to the female spouse. Additionally, among high-paid women, there is no evidence of a significant shift towards male spouses staying at home, even part-time, to manage the private sphere.[26] Women in leadership positions are much less likely to be married than their male counterparts and are less likely to have children than their male counterparts of the same age or than women in general of the same age.[27] Over one third of elite women business leaders are childless and, of the rest, only 14.7% have more than two children. On the other hand, 91.6% of male business leaders have children.[28] Part-time working offers an opportunity for women to combine childcare and domestic responsibilities with a professional career. However, it is often not available to women at the top of their profession. There is, therefore, considerable evidence that elite women in general and women accountants in particular, experience work-life balance barriers to their progression that their male counterparts do not.

Let us now consider the phenomenon that women are more likely to exercise personal choice to 'bale out' of the partnership track than men.

WOMEN CHOOSING TO 'BALE OUT' OR 'QUIT'

In spite of the obstacles, there are women who succeed in overcoming barriers and in making it to the top of the profession. However, there is evidence that elite women are more likely to opt out, or quit the partnership track than elite men. Women who succeed in overcoming the barriers mentioned above have a higher propensity to abandon the top jobs than their male counterparts. This is true in senior executive positions generally.[29] More specifically, the major accountancy firms have difficulty in retaining women in senior positions.[30] It would seem that there is no gender difference in the numbers quitting due to the competitive environment, increasing litigation, or salary levels. However, women are significantly more likely to leave due to work/non-work

---

* The term 'spouse' will be used to indicate a life partner in order to avoid confusion with the term 'partner' which is used to denote the job title.

pressures and women are more likely to leave professional practice for industry due to the stress associated with practice.[31] The tension between work and home responsibilities is also a factor driving more women to 'bale out' than men.[32]

A recent study which is not specific to accountants, but relates to women who had quit their high-powered, well-paid, professional jobs, found that women leave due to a complex range of reasons which include:

- In spite of an array of life-work-balance and family friendly policies, the women found that their jobs were inflexible in practice. While there may have been policies to support part-time working, for example, they found themselves unable to avail of this arrangement at their level. Even when they did, they experienced 'hours creep' which brought them back up to the hours previously worked.
- Their 60-hour work week and 24/7 availability with extensive travel were just not sustainable alongside family commitments.
- They experienced uncontrollable deadlines and found that the 'mommy track' designed by their employers simply derailed their careers and marked them as uninterested in competing for promotion.
- They experienced exhaustion and burnout.
- They described an effective motherhood bar and spoke of the ideal worker as 'unencumbered by family' and having a stay-at-home wife.
- Many planned to turn to teaching/training as more likely to accommodate their needs.[33]

Summary

Women are not making it to the top professional posts in the same proportion as their male colleagues. They experience gender-specific barriers and they are quitting the profession in greater numbers than men. The organisational culture in professional accounting firms is *workaholic* and the philosophy is 'up or out'.[34] The Big Four accounting firms are having difficulty in retaining women at a high level.

They are not losing them to the home, but to other employment which allows them to continue their careers in balance with their other life commitments.

The barriers described in this chapter can be classified into organisational and personal, with some being attributable to workplace policies and culture and others deriving from the women's own career ambitions and decisions about how they want to balance their lives. However, there is no doubt that, whatever the causes, there is a force that draws women more than men away from the professional practice of accountancy into other career paths and those women who stay are obliged to find mechanisms for coping with those forces. The loss of their valuable skills and competencies is undoubtedly a cause for concern.

The research heretofore that examined the career progression of women in the accountancy profession has focussed on two areas: identification of the barriers and obstacles that women experience in breaking the glass ceiling and a description of the flight from the top, or women 'opting out' once they make it to the top. This book takes a reconstructivist rather than a deconstructivist standpoint. In other words, instead of focussing on the negative aspects of the barriers to and the flight of women, it examines the issue of elite women from a more positive perspective. Hence, rather than engaging in a critique of the current situation for women and deconstructing the environment to explore the problems, the next chapters concentrate on the experiences of elite women who have recognised and overcome the barriers and obstacles, who have been promoted to the elite positions in the profession and who have stayed. If feminism is a political activity, it is suggested that a good contribution can be made by exploring the characteristics of those women who have succeeded to see if any common themes emerge that can be used to:

- inform the cohort of young women who are currently on the career path upwards;
- advise the professional firms as they construct work practices and cultures to identify and mentor future partners; and
- hold up a mirror to elite women in accountancy as they reflect on the lives they have sculpted for themselves.

REFERENCES

1. Walby S. (1997), *Theorizing Patriarchy*, Basil Blackwell, Oxford.
2. Barker P. and Monks K. (1998), Irish Women Accountants and Career Progression, *Accounting, Organisations and Society*, Vol. 23, No. 8, pp 813–823.
3. For more discussion of this phenomenon of blending in rather than standing out, see Sinclair A. (1999), *Doing Leadership Differently*, Melbourne University Press, Australia.
4. This exploitation by women of women specific market business opportunities has been explored by writers such as: Banner L. (1983), *American Beauty*, Knopf, New York; Walsh M. (1992), Plush Endeavours: an Analysis of the Modern American Soft-toy Industry, *Business History Review*, no. 66, Winter pp 637–670; Peiss K. (1998), *Hope in a Jar: the Making of America's Beauty Culture*, Metropolitan Books, New York; and Willet J. (2000), *Permanent Waves, the Making of the American Beauty Shop*, New York University Press, New York.
5. Rosenthal P. (1995), Gender Differences in Managers – Attributions for Successful Work Performance, *Women in Management Review*, Vol. 10, No. 6, pp 26–31, for a discussion of this issue and of the unique tendency that women have to explain away their successes and to take personal blame for their failures.
6. See, for a discussion of these issues and for the finding that women often display an external locus of control: O'Connor V. (2001), Women and Men in Senior Management – a "Different Needs" Hypothesis, *Women in Management Review*, Vol. 16, No. 8, pp 400–404; and White B., Cox C., and Cooper C. (1997), A Portrait of Successful Women, *Women in Management Review*, Vol. 12, No. 1, pp 27–34.
7. For further reading on the transactional and transformational styles of leadership, see: Avolio B, Bass B., and Jung D. (1999), Re-examining the Components of Transformational and Transactional Leadership Using the Multifactor Leadership Questionnaire, *Journal of Occupational and Organizational Psychology*, Vol. 72, pp 441–462; Eagly A. (2007), Female Leadership – Advantage and Disadvantage: Resolving the Contradictions, *Psychology of Women Quarterly*, 31, pp 1–12; Alimo-Metcalfe, B. and Alban-Metcalf (2003), *Leadership: a Masculine Past, but a Feminine Future?* Paper presented to the annual BPS Occupational Psychology Conference, August 2003.
8. Metcalf B. and Linstead A. (2003) Gendering Teamwork: Re-writing the Feminine, *Gender Work and Organization*, Vol. 10, No. 1.
9. Ely R. (1994), The Social Construction of Relationships among Professional Women at Work, in Davidson M. and Burke R. (eds), *Women in Management, Current Research Issues*, Paul Chapman, London.
10. For further reading on this issue see Eagly A. (ibid.), and Schneider B. (1987), The People make the Place, *Personnel Psychology*, No. 40, 437–453.
11. De Beauvoir S. (1949), *La Deuxieme Sexe, translated 1953*, Parshley H., David Campbell Publishers, London, p. 281.

12. Schein V. (1973), The Relationship between Sex Role Stereotypes and Requisite Management Characteristics, *Journal of Applied Psychology*, Vol. 57, pp 95–100; and Rosen B. and Jerdee T. (1978), Perceived Sex Differences in Managerially Relevant Characteristics, *Sex Roles*, Vol. 4, pp 837–843.
13. Eagly, ibid.
14. Hopfl H. and Sumahon M., (2007), "The Lady Vanishes", Some thoughts on Women and Leadership, *Journal of Organizational Change Management*, Vol. 20, No. 2, pp 198–208.
15. See, for example, Wellington S., Kroof M., and Gerkovich P., (2003), What is Holding Women Back? *Harvard Business Review*, June, Vol. 81, Issue 6, pp 18–21.
16. Lyness et al. (2003).
17. Palgi M. (2000), *Top People and Mentors in Gendering Elites*, Vianello and Moore, Macmillan Press, Basingstoke.
18. Palgi, ibid.
19. Liddle J. and Michielsens E. (2000), Gender, Class and Public Power, in *Gendering Elites*, Vianello and Moore, Macmillan Press, Basingstoke.
20. Nicolau-Smotoviti and Baldwin (2000), ibid.
21. Ramli A. (2002), *Challenges Facing the Women Accountants in the New Millennium*, Akauntan Nasioinal, May.
22. Barker P., and Monks (1998), ibid.
23. Barker P. and Monks (1998), ibid.
24. Woodward A., and Lyon D. (2000), Gendered Time and Women's Access to Power, in *Gendering Elites*, Vianello and Moore, Macmillan Press, Basingstoke.
25. Bacik et al. (2003), ibid.
26. Diem-Willie G., and Ziegler J. (2000), Traditional and New Ways of Living, in *Gendering Elites*, Vianello and Moore, Macmillan Press, Basingstoke.
27. Davidson M. and Cooper C., (1992), *Shattering the Glass Ceiling: The Woman Manager*, Paul Chapman, London. (See also, Neale (2000))
28. Neale (2000), ibid.
29. Schwartz F. (1998), Management Women and the New Facts of Life, *Harvard Business Review*, Jan/Feb pp 65–76.
30. Dalton D. and Hill J. (1997), Women as Managers and Partners, *Auditing*, Spring, Vol. 16, Issue 1, pp 29–53.
31. Collins K. (1993), Stress and Departures from the Public Accounting Profession: A Study of Gender Differences, *Accounting Horizons*, March, Vol. 7, No. 1, pp 29–38.
32. Bagihole B. (2002), *Women in Non-Traditional Occupations – Challenging Men*, Palgrave Macmillan, Basingstoke.
33. Stone P. (2007), *Opting Out? Why Women Really Quit Careers and Head Home*, University of California Press, Berkeley.
34. Hooks and Cheramy (1994).

4

♦

HEARING THE VOICES FROM
THE GLASS CEILING

Who are the women who overcome the barriers to success in the accountancy profession? What kind of women makes it to partnership in one of the Big Four firms? Are there any common themes running through their personal qualities and their backgrounds? How did they make it to partnership and how did they navigate their course around the barriers? How did they manage their lives having achieved partnership?

In this and the next chapter, I describe the research that I conducted with 43 women partners in the Big Four firms in English-speaking countries. They agreed to tell their stories and reflect on their experiences so that others might benefit. In this chapter I explain the methodology used and summarise the interviewees' significant personal characteristics and backgrounds[*] and then, in Chapter 5, I describe how they managed their careers, and overcame the obstacles.

THE RESEARCH METHODOLOGY

I adopted a two-stage approach. First, in order to format the structure of the interviews, I wanted to pinpoint the significance of key aspects of the women's background and experience, from their perspective and from the perspective of their male peers. So I undertook

---

[*] For an unabridged version of the full research report, please contact the author at the Institute of Chartered Accountants in Ireland.

both a pilot study and a focus group. Secondly, I conducted detailed interviews with 43 women who are partners. I used a qualitative approach, rather than a quantitative one, because of the small number of women partners in the firms and because no such previous study exists to provide a clear hypothesis to test. The results of this research enable us to see through the eyes of the elite women themselves, allowing the themes to emerge from their experiences.

Pilot Study

A pilot study, in the form of a short questionnaire, was firstly sent to all the women partners in the Big Four firms in Ireland in order to:

1. Introduce the study to them;
2. Obtain a preliminary view from them of what they think are the most significant elements contributing to their success; and
3. Explore the possibility that they display predominantly masculine characteristics in order to address the suggestion (mentioned earlier) that elite women have to behave like men or exhibit masculine characteristics in order to succeed. This issue was tested using the Bem Inventory method to measure their psychological androgyny, femininity or masculinity.[1]

There were 17 usable responses to this pilot study out of 19 questionnaires sent. The factors which respondents identified as having high impact on their success were:

*   their own self-motivation,
*   their technical abilities,
*   the support of family and spouse,
*   having a strong mentor within the firm,
*   being a highly competitive person, and
*   having had a good education.

The outcome of administering Bem's test to the 17 participants is shown in Table 4.1. The test classified the women as Feminine (displaying largely feminine responses), Masculine (displaying largely masculine responses), Androgynous (with a high score on both masculine and feminine responses) or Undifferentiated (with scores below the medians on both masculine and feminine items).

Table 4.1 Classification of Irish women partners

Classification	Number	%
Feminine	0	0
Androgynous	2	12
Undifferentiated	3	17
Masculine	12	71
Total	17	100

These outcomes, indicating the factors perceived as having had an impact on their success and the very high incidence of masculinity, determined the scope of the detailed interviews in exploring the experience of the women in their early life, through their education, in their family life and into the profession to trace their experience with their career progression and their perception of their own characteristics.

Focus Group

In order to give some balance to the perspective of the themes emerging and to ensure that no obvious omissions had been made, I also convened a focus group with eight male partners from the Big Four firms to explore their views, on a confidential basis, about women-specific characteristics they observed in their women partners. The objective was to hear their views on the issue of women entering this previously all-male preserve and to provide me with a context in hearing the experiences of the women. Their input provided a form of assurance that hearing the voices of solely women partners did not result in the exclusion of some significant theme.

Amongst the men, there was broad agreement in their perceptions of the differences between women and men partners insofar as they existed. The eight members of the focus group reached broad agreement in relation to some commonalities they observed in their women partners. Using their own terminology, they largely concurred that their women partners were:

- extremely 'hot' on the technical detail – better than the men;
- better at 'getting on very well' with their staff;
- better at handling the HR issues in the firm;
- very reliable and could be trusted not to 'chance their arm';
- more likely to be 'sticky' about a technical point, for example, in saying to the client "You cannot do that" rather than finding a commercial solution;
- less likely to socialise with the client;
- more likely to attract adverse comments from the client that they are less flexible and more difficult to deal with than the male partners. They are less likely to 'negotiate around the needs of the client' than the male partners;
- more likely to carry on insisting on their perspective longer than their male partners – taking up time and delaying a deal;
- likely to attract the annoyance of their male partners when they go off on maternity leave when 'someone else has to carry the load for them' and then, 'no sooner are they back, than they are off again on maternity leave';
- not given as much weight for their arguments in partners' meetings if they are only part-time.

The comments above indicate both favourable and adverse observations. The overwhelming view expressed at the focus group meeting was, however, that women partners add to the diversity of the firm and that there should be more of them to create a better balance, although there was an underlying contradictory sense that it would really be better if they could be more like a man. There were feelings of resentment around maternity leave, part-time working, and not socialising enough with the client. Additionally, the reference to not being sufficiently 'flexible' in finding 'commercial solutions' for the client implied that the male partners are flexible and there was an unspoken inference that these issues could be corrected if women responded more like men in some of these areas. The discussion provided useful perceptions against which to hear the women's voices. However, this was just a focus group to give balance to the major objective of hearing the women's voices, and the question of cross-gender perceptions may warrant further fruitful study.

THE INTERVIEWS

Building on the foundation provided by both the pilot study and the focus group, the form of interview was determined and meetings were arranged with the women partners who participated in this study.[†] The objective of those interviews was to allow me to hear and probe new clues and to secure vivid, accurate and inclusive accounts of the women's personal experiences. In turn, the interviews facilitated their reflection on their lives, influences and experiences and the extent to which such factors as well as their personal characteristics contributed to their success in reaching and holding their elite positions.

The subject matter is personal and confidential, both in respect of the women themselves and their firms, and so their names and the firms they work with have been withheld. All the women have been given fictitious names, and the report of their observations is given under those fictitious names.

Interviewees included women partners in Big Four firms in Dublin, Sydney, Melbourne, Cape Town, Johannesburg, Wellington and Boston. This was not a study to identify any international or firm-based differences. In fact, the Big Four firms are global entities and have similar policies and standards ensuring that all the interviewees would have experienced a similar progression track to partnership. The use of other English-speaking environments allowed me to interview a larger number than would have been possible had the research been restricted to Ireland. However, it is interesting to note that no significant cultural

---

[†] If you are interested in reading the technical details of the research methodology, please contact the author at Chartered Accountants Ireland.

differences emerged and the findings were similar across all geographic locations.

The range and profile of the interviewees is summarised in Tables 4.2, 4.3 and 4.4.

Table 4.2 Age profile of interviewees

Age					
Years	20 – 30	31 – 40	41 – 50	51 – 60	Total
Number of interviewees	1	18	18	6	43
%	2	42	42	14	100

Table 4.3 Number of children interviewees had

Number of children					
Number of children	0	1	2	3	4
Number of interviewees with this number of children	19	6	11	6	1
%	45	14	25	14	2
Mean age of interviewees with this number of children	41	41	40	45	52

Table 4.4 Marital status of interviewees

Marital status				
Status	Single	Married	Divorced	Total
Number of interviewees	10	27	6	43
%	23	63	14	100

For completeness it should be noted that only one interviewee indicated that she was gay and only one interviewee was a woman of colour (not the same woman). The issues of the percentage of gay people and of people of colour who make partnership could be areas of interest for further research.

How Could these Elite Women Be Described?

The principal findings from the interviews can be grouped into the following themes:

- Personal characteristics of the women
- Their personal background } (see Chapter 4)
- How they managed their careers
- Their capacity to overcome barriers and obstacles } (see Chapter 5)
- Active career planning

Personal Characteristics

Self-confidence

On first acquaintance, the interviewees all presented as very professional. Most wore smart and expensive business suits with varying degrees of style. They wore subdued accessories and shoes, with minimal make-up and discreet and expensive jewellery. They generally had well-cut hair and well-manicured hands. They appeared self-confident and business-like and seemed well-organised and well-supported in their offices. They appeared to fit the model of successful partner in a fairly conservative profession. In describing themselves during the course of the interviews, they referred to the necessity to appear self-confident. Sue's observation was typical:

> *You have to be confident in what you are saying in order to work with the clients at the level of the people that I'm dealing with. You can't be wishy-washy. (Sue)*

However, many of the interviewees made a surprising disclosure that, inside, they did not feel the level of self-confidence that they knew they had to project. Rachel's comment was representative:

> *I come across very confidently. I don't think I'm as confident as people think. Well, I know I'm not as confident as people think and I'm far more sensitive than people think as well. It's almost like I have this veneer on the outside and I think I've had that for many years and I think that it's a self protection, it's a defence barrier. (Rachel)*

There was a strong and often repeated reference to self-doubt, and a fear that it was due to some terrible mistake that they had been promoted to such a high level. Some referred to the need for reassurance that their work was good, although they realised that, at partner level, it was unlikely to be forthcoming. However, through the niggling self-questioning, many could see quite clearly that, when they compared themselves rationally with their peers, they were as good as, if not better than, others who projected themselves with supreme self-confidence almost to the point of arrogance. They found inner reserve to reassure themselves. Norma's comment was pertinent for most of the interviewees:

> I mean there's obviously self-doubt and I think a lot of people and even the most successful women will say to you "I don't actually know how I got here and somebody's going to find out that I'm a fraud one day". But I guess you must demonstrate your ability along the way and tap into your inner belief in your own ability. I guess I always used to just look at the people ahead of me and think "Well if they can do it, I can do it." You know, I'm just as good as they are! (Norma)

This was a very honest and revealing disclosure. The women reflected that it was doubtful whether their male partners experience the same level of self-analysis and self-doubt. The need for structured reflection, possibly with a peer mentor or a network group seemed apparent. However, having come through a period (pre-partnership) of very highly controlled and managed career planning, mentoring, review and tracking, the women partners experienced the sudden end of the formal career planning and mentoring at a time when they felt the need for support and assurance most strongly, i.e. after election to partnership.

Male characteristics

The women were conscious that they were working in a male-dominated environment at the top of the firms. Some referred to having to operate in a 'blokey' environment and having to fit in by displaying 'blokey' characteristics themselves. Victoria typified the often-repeated view that they needed to be better than their male competitors to be elected to partnership:

> *If you work hard, you can compete with the blokes, but usually you have to outperform them to be accepted. (Victoria)*

There were numerous references to feeling that they were like men in many of their characteristics. Some felt they were always like that, and others just adapted to the male environment in which they found themselves. Some women, like Ann, Delia and Linda, thought that it was a natural and long-standing preference for them to display more male characteristics:

> *I think generally I have some male tendencies. I don't think people who look at me think I look male – more tomboy. I am not very adventurous, but I think, on balance, I think more like a man, and have always done so. I am afraid to use the word logical, that makes it sound like women are illogical, but I do go through a thought process more like a man than a woman. (Ann)*

> *I have been told that I look feminine, but I have a lot of masculine characteristics. (Delia)*

> *They call me 'the scary lady' around here. I wouldn't describe myself as a girly girl. (Linda)*

Others, like Norma, felt that they had simply played the game necessary to fit in:

> *I was in a mainly male class in university and I guess that's had influences on how you can modify your behaviours in professional life to suit the situation that you're in. (Norma)*

However, a small number of respondents, like Loreta, spoke of their responses as characteristically female:

> *I guess I'm probably the type of person, being female, who can juggle more than one thing at once and is diligent and organised. I am also not a very aggressive person at all and I look at guys who are my peers. If they get upset or angry they project their anger with their presence whereas I would just cry. I'll get upset and sit in my office.*

I guess I'm sort of probably more of a consensus girl in not wanting to create waves. (Loreta)

In spite of displaying masculine characteristics, this 'cry' response was experienced by several of the women. Often, however, even if they wanted to 'have a good bawl' about some disagreement or conflict, the women talked of going to a private place – their office or car or to the bathroom – before allowing the tears to flow. It was suggested that a masculine display of emotion (shouting and displaying anger), was more acceptable than a feminine display of emotion (crying).

Interviewees identified self-marketing or what Colleen described as 'blowing one's own trumpet' as a masculine trait that was necessary for promotion and recognition, but one which they and other women, even if they display other masculine characteristics, find hard to adopt. Many of the interviewees mentioned that they were not good at self-marketing their achievements. Typically, they would see their male colleagues as better at this activity than themselves. They assumed that their achievements spoke for themselves and they did not feel comfortable drawing the attention of their colleagues and assessors to them. Liz gave a good example when she described her reaction when she felt she deserved promotion, but it did not seem to be forthcoming:

I may have left at that point, if they had not made the move, because I am not a pushy kind of person. I was not going to say: "If you don't make me a partner, I'm leaving." I think I was more of the kind of person, probably still am, who feels "If you can't see the value in me, I'm not going to go and yell, shout and scream until you take notice of me. My acts or my results will speak for themselves." (Liz)

Jo and Linda articulated the difference in how women operate and the difficulty in trying to manage the domestic and public sphere, while often doing a better job than the 'guys' and doing it quietly and stoically and not making their successes known:

No one appreciates how difficult it is for a professional woman. They're still looking after themselves which is a hell of a lot bloody harder work than a man who's married and gets his shirts ironed and washed and his dinner on the table when he gets home at night and, you know, slippers out for you and all that sort of stuff. She still has to turn out a first class professional job. It all varies obviously but I think women aren't so much into selling themselves. (Jo)

I think women achieve things and they don't bang on about it. When they have done a good job, they expect someone to notice that they have done a good job, but they really don't expect to strut around like a peacock. I think they form relationships in different ways, I think their clients end up trusting them, because they are looked after. I suspect they are not as good at the flattery as the men. (Linda)

It seems likely, therefore, that it is helpful for women who want to become partners to demonstrate male characteristics in the male environment of the partnership track. The male partners who took part in the focus group expressed a desire, albeit somewhat confused, to have diversity, and recognised the importance of the characteristics that women can add to good decision-making and management. However, if the way many women operate comfortably is not understood or valued, smart women will adapt to that which is valued. This means that there will be a tendency to promote to partnership those women who demonstrate mainly male characteristics, either because it is most natural for them or because they are prepared to adopt those characteristics since it is the preferred currency. This can result in having the partnership profile mainly masculine even when it comprises men and women.

If the preponderant-characteristic at the top is masculine, it is difficult to provide a feminine mentoring model for the younger women who are coming up through the firm. So, many excellent women, who do not wish to 'play the game', or who have few role models, will leave the firm and will be lost to the partnership. Additionally, women who have adopted male characteristics may be left with a residual feeling of stress since they are uncomfortable with parts of the role they play.

Independence

Many of the interviewees spoke of their financial and professional independence and clearly felt that they did not wish to be dependent financially on anyone else. As Gillian and Jane explained:

I was born like this ... I have been like this as far back as I can remember, fiercely independent about everything. I don't think I am independent because I can be, I think I am independent because I have the desire to look after myself. (Gillian)

When my son was born and I was trying to do everything on my own, it was part of the reason why I didn't seek more help. It wasn't that I couldn't afford to get help. It was that I could be able to show that I could do everything, and I was this superwoman. (Jane)

In excess of one in four of the interviewees spoke of a childhood memory of financially straitened circumstances which they feel impacted on their need to have financial independence and to earn sufficient income to provide a very strong financial cushion. Some examples of the stories they told included:

I think my upbringing and my background is really important because as a child we didn't have holidays. We didn't have lots of … yummy things. What I feel very strongly about now is that I want my children to have a good education, holiday…. We have a beach house and I'm going to continue to work for a period of time that allows us to have financial security and we as a family not just the children but we as a family can enjoy it because that is really important to me now. It's not that I am materialistic, it's financial security to enable me and us to give things to our children. (Rachel)

I had to get high enough grades to get a five hundred dollar book prize, then to get a one thousand dollar scholarship, cobble together the two or three thousand dollars tuition for the year and paid for a little hovel to live in. So I had a period of having to struggle for money. But that was a grey period. I don't want to go there again. (Miriam)

I guess when we came [here] we didn't have very much – you know nine suitcases and five hundred dollars for a family of four so we had to start from scratch. So I think it was all linked, it wasn't purely financial versus education but my parents were very keen for us to be properly educated so we can then use that and succeed in life. I feel that I do not want to be worried about money and I like the income associated with this job. (Aisling)

We had one dress each outside of school. We had one pair of shoes that weren't our school shoes. We were the poorest kids in the school by a country mile but we were getting the best education. And then, when I was about 14, my mother left my father which was a pretty unusual thing to do in the mid-1970s. I was the eldest child and my mother had no sense of money and I think I got left with a lot of responsibility for paying electricity bills and managing the finances for the family as well as it being drummed into us that you've got to be independent and you should never rely on a man for your income. I think that drumming in of the independence and the encouragement always to strive to do your best academically are the two things that probably gave me a determination and independence that is where I am today. (Jo)

During my childhood, I wouldn't have had financial security and I would have watched my mother struggling to make the money stretch. When I was very young we struggled for every pencil at school. So I think I have a financial driver, which my own children don't have. You have to go out to work and make money and provide security. Financial security would have been a big thing with me. (Priscilla)

I would be careful with money and that comes from a period in my life when I can remember hiding upstairs when the milkman came and we didn't have the money to pay him. (Ann)

There were five kids in my family and money was very tough. Money is very important to me now. I often recall the rooting in pockets to find coins to buy some bread and I never want that to happen to me. (Yvonne)

I always thought that I would have a secure well earning job behind me and that would have been very important to me, the security and the fact that there was a reasonable amount of money involved. That just comes from the family background. I felt we were always scrimping. (Jane)

These women earn a significant amount of money. For many of them, the financial reward is really important. The security of not having to rely on anyone else and the capacity to provide the kind of things for their children that they did not have are noteworthy drivers for them. This financial reward is so important to them that the price of the long hours, the separation from children and the reduction of time for themselves and friends, are prices worth paying.

For many other women, however, the marginal value of an additional €10,000 in income becomes less valuable beyond a particular point and the value of time off and a more balanced life style becomes greater. Some of the women partners, while they enjoyed the income, referred to reaching a point when they would prefer some more time off instead of financial increments.

Competitiveness

Being a competitive person was a characteristic that was mentioned by many of the interviewees. Daisy, for example, compared herself to other women managers in the firm when they were on the partnership track. She distinguished herself by her competitiveness. Jo and Brenda were honest in acknowledging that being competitive is something that women often deny about themselves, and Sarah suggested that, for her, competition was not beating others, but beating her own objectives:

> But I would admit I was more driven than some of the others, ambitious and competitive and focused on the future and a little bit more materialistic. I am an action person not a reflective person. (Daisy)

> I think I'm quite competitive … in a funny sense, I look at myself now playing sport and don't have to win … but when it comes to work I have to be the best at it, I try really hard to consciously tell myself it doesn't matter. (Jo)

> I keep saying to my friends, I'm not competitive. They just laugh at me so I guess I really must be. (Brenda)

> I'm not competitive with other people, but, unlike the guys, I'm competitive with myself. In other words I'm not fazed by somebody being promoted over me - or I might feel a little twinge, and cross about it for a while - but my values are, I judge myself against myself, so when I fail, I fail myself. (Sarah)

The issue of being competitive as a prerequisite for partnership was identified in the pilot study and confirmed throughout the interviews. A number of the women reflected that naked competitiveness is not an attractive quality in a woman. However, they accepted that to succeed at partnership, candidates need to be willing to compete fairly forcefully with the other aspirants. This is undoubtedly the same for male candidates. The difference is that women are competing in a field where they are uncomfortable (as discussed earlier) in self-marketing themselves. The tactic of competing against themselves rather than overtly competing against others appears, from these interviews, to be one that women adopt more than men. It is important for the gate-keepers who are promoting and voting on potential partnership candidates to understand this difference and to factor it into their decision-making.

Intelligent and academic achiever

It was clear from the interviews that, with very few exceptions, the interviewees had been high achievers at school and later at university and/or in the professional examinations.

> *A friend of mine from school who I had lost touch with, met my sister and they said: "Oh what is she doing now?". When she heard I was a partner here, she was impressed but not surprised. She said: "Well, she was always very driven and an achiever." (Daisy)*

Surprise at realising that they were bright and high achievers recurred again and again. It was almost as if, when they scored well at examination, they had a deep-seated fear that it would emerge that a mistake had been made. Examples included:

> *There was a bunch in school and they were all very good, but I knew I was as good and better, so that drove me. But every exam I ever sat I always thought I failed, which I never did. I generally came top of the class, but it was a constant surprise to me. (Gillian)*

> *I got a first and was offered places by five of the Big Six, which was a big surprise for me, as I always felt that my exam results were something of a matter of chance rather than talent although I worked*

very hard and would have been disappointed if I had failed at any stage. (Orna)

I was surprised, but began to realise that I probably was quite a bright person. (Melanie)

I really had no idea how good I was at school or college and genuinely felt surprised when I did well at examinations. (Ann)

I sometimes think that I am not really supposed to be a partner. It was just a mistake and I will soon be found out. (Aisling)

To be a partner, it is important to be smart and to have demonstrated intellectual capacity. This is true for male and female candidates for partnership. What may be different is the sense of surprise the women feel when their intelligence is recognised. This may be linked to the expressed lower self-confidence women experience. Again, this re-enforces the need to incorporate an understanding of this difference in the firm's support, assessment, and mentoring systems to ensure that potentially good women are not excluded or do not self-exclude from the progression process.

Personal Background

The women had a wide range of personal backgrounds, as would be expected. In reviewing the backgrounds, some common themes emerged.

Traumas

A significant minority (more than one third) of the interviewees spoke about personal difficulties they had to contend with as they were growing up. The majority, however, came from stable and happy families that offered important support to the interviewees. The respondents who experienced trauma have managed their careers and have succeeded in attaining the very top of their profession in spite of the personal sadness that is still present for them. Many spoke of the strong awareness of their trauma, but they have developed coping styles to allow them to progress in their careers notwithstanding the pain. A sample of the personal stories includes:

My father died. I found it hard to cope with that loss, but my mother did not want his death to interfere with my career and so I sat the professional exams on the morning he was buried and she postponed the funeral until the afternoon. . It took me a long time to ... even comprehend that decision, but I accepted that was where she was coming from. (Ann)

When I was 12 I had to grow up very quickly, my 10-year-old brother died and it was extremely tragic. (Gillian)

My father died when I was 11. (Jo)

My parents actually separated when I was ten and my brother took it really hard for a long time. So from the age of about 11 I started doing a lot of family household things because Mum went out to work full-time to look after three children so I was doing all the cooking and cleaning and all those things when I was going to school. (Rachel)

We knew we were going to 'Uni' and we weren't going to rely on our parents we were actually going to pay our own way. So I left home at eighteen but was really finding it emotionally difficult. My Dad was drinking. It was something that wasn't talked about, I found myself sleep-walking while I was in my first year of Uni. (Miriam)

The other relevant thing was that my mother got cancer when I was 12 or 13 and I became the principal worker at home, my older sister married very young and my brother was gone out of the picture in terms of doing any running of the house. (Jane)

My mother was a limiting influence. We never did any sport, because my mother always had a baby and she needed us always to be around. So we would go to school and she would drop us off and collect us and when we went home, we did our chores for the day. It was a very closed family; we never had much freedom to do other activities or to have friends. (Betty)

The conclusion to be drawn from conversation with the women who had experienced personal trauma was that it is not imperative to have a 'normal', stable, nuclear family background in order to succeed. What was common among these women was that they confronted their sadness and had the capacity to talk about it freely.

Profile of parents and family

These interviews indicate no pattern in the background of either parent or of the number of siblings. Interviewees ranged from being an only child to having up to six siblings; some were the eldest and some the youngest with some in the middle, but with no particular pattern emerging. Fathers' jobs ranged from the professional, including engineers, academics and one accountant, to farmers to clerical workers to business owners. The strongest pattern to emerge was that of the mother working in the home. However, given the age profile of the respondents, it is to be expected that, since the majority of women at that time ceased work on marriage or on motherhood, it would be reflected in this study. The majority of mothers were employed full-time in the home, but some were teachers, secretaries/clerical, business owners and one fashion buyer.

> *I am the eldest child as well that would have been probably a reason why I was so ambitious for myself. (Delia)*

> *I was in the middle of seven children in my family and had noisy siblings either side of me and I developed a pretty good technique of keeping my head down and getting on with my own things while my brothers and sister seemed to get into trouble a lot. (Collette)*

Support of parents

Most of the women, including those who had experienced the loss of one parent, recalled parents who were supportive but not pushy. The parents, taking into account the views of their daughter, established what her objectives were and supported those objectives. They did not appear to decide for their daughter and push her down the route they decided. The emphasis was on what their daughter thought would make her happy and what her capability was and then supporting her in her decision with an emphasis on providing the best possible education:

> *My parents always said: "We will support you however much you want to do, as far as you want to go to the very best of your ability". And I think you kind of pick that stuff up from your folks and that does make a difference. (Daisy)*

> *My Mum was very good at encouraging myself and my sister and brother in terms of 'reach your full potential, do whatever you can in terms of your capabilities'. My father was very much the same in terms of his view on life. When we were going through school, they were very good at giving counsel about subjects to select, not telling me what to do but asking me why and what would that lead to and how would that help me and very open sort of questions in terms of direction. (Gladys)*

> *My parents were always very good at saying: "You should do what you're good at and what makes you happy." So I guess their message was be happy as an individual and if that means University and a profession that's great, if it doesn't that's fine too. (Loretta)*

> *My parents would have been of the view that if you are happy, then do what makes you happy. (Priscilla)*

> *My parents didn't know too much about accountancy, but they were very keen on education and gave me lots of praise whenever I achieved anything. I always felt that they would give me praise (although not financial or other reward like my friends) but not criticise if I tried something and failed. (Victoria)*

> *It was a really happy childhood and we were encouraged to reach for the sun and the moon and do the very best we could at everything. There was always competition between us in school and at things like sports and swimming and riding, but we were always made to believe that it was wonderful that we took part and nice, but not specially wonderful to come first. (Orna)*

These themes of parental support, regular praise and focus on working to the top of one's ability range recurred throughout the interviews. It would appear that their competitiveness came from within rather than from a driven parent. This finding may be too late for those who are already on the partnership track, as they have left their childhood, but it is pertinent for all of us who are or might be parents.

THE ROLE OF EDUCATION

As observed above, many of the interviewees recalled the importance placed on education by their parents. The interviewees themselves reflected on their own education. The strong recurring themes that emerged were having been educated in single sex schools (many in Catholic convents), having been academically strong, specifically at mathematics, and having been resistant to the gender stereotype. There was occasional mention of friendship in school. However, it was not a recurring theme and there was no mention of network building at school or university.

Single-sex education

Most of the respondents had been to single-sex schools right up to and throughout their secondary education, and two had been to all-women colleges at university. Of the single-sex schools, most were run by religious orders. Although one interviewee expressed a preference for co-education, the majority who had been through single-sex education had good memories and were good students who had a good experience which they would recommend to others. Sarah articulated a widely held view:

> *I would favour all-girl schools for girls. I think that boys and girls learn differently, and at different stages, and I think it's unfair to put the boys with the girls. I think little girls are more academic, they are happier to sit and read and write and they are much quieter physically, they don't have as much energy as boys. So they will be ahead of boys, and it will make the boys feel disadvantaged, in their early years when they are learning to read and write, because the girls are ahead of them, and then they get very discouraged, and*

then also, little boys are very irritating. They are very busy, and have lots of energy and they distract the little girls who want to sit and do their own thing, so I put both my children into single sex schools. (Sarah)

Academic attainment at third level

Most interviewees were graduates and, with few exceptions, very good academically at third level. Where they did not have sufficient resources to fund their education, many attracted scholarships and grants or had to work to fund themselves. Some mentioned that there were few others in their class who succeeded in getting to university. Many mentioned particular lecturers or teachers who had a significant influence on their success. Nearly all interviewees also enjoyed their time at university.

I came through with very good results but I didn't leave it to chance. I did study hard at University to make sure that I got top results and my professional exams were the same. I was very careful to make sure that I got good marks. (Deirdre)

I studied economics and politics and got a first and really had no problems getting a job. (Collette)

Resistant to the gender stereotype

Although some interviewees referred to their teachers as being good role models for girls and to their schools as having an ethos of encouraging girls to reach for the stars and to become anything they wanted, the overriding recollection was that of a clear gender stereotype of girls as housewives, teachers and clerical workers, a stereotype that the interviewees consciously resisted.

The career guidance I got was you should go into the bank or civil service, you should become a teacher maybe. I was one of only three who ended up going to university. (Jane)

My extended family didn't encourage females to progress too far because they said it was a waste when you are only going to stay at home and have a family. (Deirdre)

When I went for an interview for accounting, the interviewer said to me if I was looking for a husband I should go to UCD because there was a much better selection. (Melanie)

So the school we were at did assume that all their students would be either teachers or nurses or housewives, and in fact about ninety-nine per cent did. (Niamh)

It is worth noting that most (but not all) of the women who encountered these gender stereotype attitudes were over 45. This may mean that our society has now moved on and all avenues are open to women – or at least that the stereotyping is more subtle than it was. What it indicates, however, is that the successful women had a strong ability to think for themselves and not to accept the societal norms.

Choice of degree route into accountancy

The most common route for the interviewees was via an undergraduate degree in Business (including Commerce, Economics or Econometrics). Next most common was an undergraduate programme in Accounting or Finance; then routes through Law, Arts, Science or Psychology. Some continued to pursue Masters programmes and some (especially some of the older women) had come straight into Articles of Clerkship from school. Once having completed their education, the reasons for choosing accountancy as a career were varied. These were:

- an interest in business, accounting and mathematics in school and college;
- an interest in the career possibilities and the financial reward attaching to accounting;
- excited by the milk round (these were mainly non-relevant graduates);
- the influence of a trusted advisor; and
- pure chance.

Summary

In summary, although the women I interviewed were very individualistic and had many differences, there were some themes that emerged. The common features that could be said to have marked them for success could be summarised as follows:

They had or were willing to adopt male characteristics. The major exception to this was their declared inability to engage in the self-marketing techniques perfected by their male colleagues.

They showed independence and they enjoyed the financial freedom that their high income gave them. They were competitive and felt that their competitiveness was innate rather than parent-induced. They were somewhat uneasy about being overly-competitive, and some rationalised this trait by pointing out that they were competing against themselves rather than against others. They were intelligent and academic high-flyers. However, they displayed a slightly ambivalent attitude to their smartness when they described, on one hand, knowing that they were as good or better than their peers and, on the other hand, being surprised when they did well at examination and assessment. This lack of self-confidence and need for reassurance aligns with their stated dislike of 'blowing their own trumpet'.

The background of the women was very varied and no common factors such as size of family, position in family, profession of father or type of schooling emerged. However, there were strong commonalities in that they nearly all went to single-sex schools, had mothers who worked full-time in the home and had supportive (but not pushy) parents. They were resistant to any societal gender stereotyping and independent enough to make up their own minds about their chosen careers.

The next chapter describes how the women partners managed their careers and overcame the obstacles and barriers.

REFERENCE

1. Bem S. L. (1975), Sex-role Adaptability: One consequence of Psychological Androgyny, *Journal of Personality and Social Psychology*, Vol. 31, pp 634–43.

5

♦

ELITE WOMEN MANAGING
THEIR CAREERS

RECOGNITION OF THE HURDLES

When the women I interviewed spoke of their experiences on the partnership track, they all referred to the challenges associated with achieving the goal of partnership. For those who were older, the partnership track seemed less structured and less clearly laid out. Those who were younger had come through the process more recently, and were much clearer about the hurdles they had to jump, the performance required and the profile necessary to be successful. They described a more transparent and independently assessed process than the older women who had come through a more penumbral journey in which the criteria were not as overtly stipulated and seemed to include, as described by Gillian, "having a face that fits".

> *The secret of success? Having a face that fits and being in the right place at the right time, with a powerful mentor. No doubt about it. (Gillian)*

All the participants spoke of the very significant rewards of partnership and their enjoyment of the challenges they faced in achieving that status. However, they also spoke of barriers to progression, some of which were common to men and women. The gender-specific barriers that they identified included:

- the difficulty in cross-gender mentoring;
- their own discomfort with networking;
- the excessive working hours; and
- the difficulty of achieving life–work balance.

HAVING A MENTOR

All the women agreed that having powerful mentors is crucial to success on the partnership track. They reported that, in recent years, the firms have introduced formal systems of allocating mentoring/counselling partners to partnership candidates. Such formal mentoring was not available to some of the older interviewees, who spoke of mentors that they had (and still have) relationships with, but under more informal arrangements. The current formal, structured mentoring system was described as reasonably well thought out in principle, but many expressed a preference, in practice, for an informal mentoring relationship. For example, Karina referred to the significance of informal mentoring by partners who "took protégées under their wing" and exposed them to powerful clients and to other partners.

As well as having an influential mentor I was very clear about having this wide network of strong partners who knew my work and had experience of working with me. (Karina)

They considered that the formal mentoring system with an allocated partner was not always a good arrangement for them, although they acknowledged that having an influential male mentor was a significant factor in their success in attaining partnership. They addressed the tension between a formal mentoring system where partners are allocated to mentees and a more informal system where partners gravitate towards mentees they identify themselves. Whilst they noted that the formal system may be more transparent, there were advantages to a system in which there is an empathy between mentor and mentee.

Aisling explained her experience:

My allocated counselling partner did not exactly work for me. I think it is better for a chemistry thing to set up the mentoring relationship. The counselling partner is meant to be looking after your career, meant to give you the feedback and the informal or formal advice along the way and then, when you come into the partnership processs, to be sponsoring you – pushing you forward. In theory, that's fine, but I found it did not work for me. (Aisling)

The interviewees had few experiences of good female mentoring, although Norma, for example, spoke of a good female mentoring relationship that had worked well for her:

> There was this female partner who made an effort to come and talk to me because the firm was making a push to promote women, but very quickly we established a great relationship, a great rapport and she in fact became a very good friend. She was somebody that I trusted and she understood exactly what I was saying and what I meant by what I was saying and sort of talked me through some of the things she'd done. And she was actually a woman whom I did hold out as a role model. Very good at the self-promoting stuff, very good at the getting what she wants, very persuasive in her arguments, very articulate, amazing client service mentality. But in other ways I didn't hold her as a role model at all, I asked her once what her priorities were, you know she said: "Work, my kids, my husband, myself"– which is all wrong to me. (Norma)

Most of the women had only male mentors. They were conscious that their lack of a good mentoring experience with a woman meant that they had missed out on an example of how they, as women, might mentor women mentees. Of course, this was largely due to the lack of women partners to fill the role of mentor for them, but Niamh offered an interesting insight into a view that many of them held that women are not good mentors for other women. When they considered themselves as mentors, interviewees often reflected that they did not regard mentoring as a significant part of their job and some, like Victoria, expressed the fairly bald view that men are better at mentoring women in the current male environment. She also reflected the generally held view that the firms should provide better training to mentors on what constitutes good mentoring.

> One of the reasons why I became a partner was I did have a male mentor and one of the reasons why I progressed quite smoothly up is that I did have male mentors. One of them was the managing partner of the firm. In my experience, women are not good mentors for women. Basically, I think it has to be [a man] not only because there's fewer females, but also you are regarded slightly suspiciously if you're pushing your own sex. And the other thing is a male can

address the other male fears, things like being taken over by women and that sort of thing. (Niamh)

Interestingly enough, of the two people I would identify as my mentors, both of them were male and to this day continue to be two of my greatest mentors. (Katy)

I have a couple of male protégés. I am not sure if I am a good mentor for the girls. The men are usually better. It is time-consuming and I am not sure I am really qualified to deal with that stuff. (Victoria)

Although in management training generally, there can be difficulties in cross-gender mentoring, these women did not refer to any problems associated with the gender of their male mentors. Any problems they spoke of were related to a clash of personality and style. The general thrust of their comments on their experience as protégées was that men were better as mentors for them and, in relation to their experience as mentors, that they felt somewhat uncomfortable mentoring younger women. This preference for a male mentor may, of course, be associated with the predominantly male characteristic of the women who make it to partnership, referred to in Chapter 4, but it presents a difficulty for young women with predominantly feminine characteristics who seek a role model similar to themselves with whom they can identify.

NETWORKING

Much of the literature refers to the failure of women to network in the same way as their male peers, and indicates that such failure can act as an obstacle to their progression.

The women I interviewed saw networking as something that they observed, but with which they were not entirely comfortable. Ann described the predicament, especially for the older partners, of not belonging to an 'old boys' network.

I suppose one of the things that was common for women at the time was that, at each incarnation of your life, you had to re-form your personal network, because it wasn't like the boys going from schools like Gonzaga or Belvedere to college who maintained their networks right through school, college and then into the profession and business. No girls went into science with me from school, so the good relationships I had in school disintegrated. Then my college friends did not transfer into business, so I had to start again. The boys had to do that to a much lesser extent. They were still surfing around with the Gonzaga or Belvedere or Clongowes brigade right through college, into the profession and now as clients. (Ann)

The interviewees in this study interpreted networking in three very distinct ways:

Networking as a form of mentoring

First, they saw it as a form of mentoring, where they 'networked' with as many partners as possible on their progression track to partnership in order to expose themselves, as described by Daisy and Aisling, to as many voting partners as possible. Rose described the importance of the extension of this form of networked delegation, and how she adapted to it even though it did not come naturally to her.

If I hadn't developed that internal network of people whom I had worked with over the years and who had seen me in all sorts of environments and tough situations, I may not have made it to partnership. I think that in a way I had to act a little bit more like a man to get there, because that network of contacts is much more a male attribute. Females tend to be more loyal to one person as opposed to consciously trying to ensure that you are working for more people, to make sure that your influence is more spread around a number of partners. I was very clear about having this wide network of influential partners who knew my work and had experience of working with me. (Daisy)

I think in my early career I was very much a single operator. I worked to one partner and I just got the work done in the quickest way and that may not necessarily involve other people. But I think when I became a senior manager and a partner I had to learn to develop the delegation, the support, the trust and networking to realise that yes, it may be hard but in the long run that's the only way you can survive is to ensure that you have that great support manager network behind you and knowing that they can cover for you when you're not available. (Rose)

I didn't think I was one of the boys but I thought I had a pretty good relationship with a number of partners because I did lots of different jobs. I had exposure to quite a few partners in the group so it wasn't a matter of one lonely voice when the partners sit down and talk about performance appraisals with their managers and senior managers. I felt that I had a good representation of partners around the table that could say: "Yeah, Aisling is doing a really good job" to counter the "No, Aisling has stuffed up". So in that regard I felt that I was good at networking with a number of partners and those partners are quite influential in the way that they would have been key to the decision-making process. (Aisling)

Networking as a form of business development

Secondly, the women saw networking as a form of business development – in socialising, playing golf, drinking with and entertaining clients. They felt that this activity does not come as easily to them as it does to most of their male partners. For example, Jo spoke of the sense of frustration when business meetings drift off into social issues. This was mirrored by the comments of the male partners in the focus group who referred to their frustration that women are not willing to engage socially with the clients in order to cement the business relationship.

In addition to their sense that it is just not appropriate to mix social engagements with business, some of the women partners, typified by Maeve's observation, felt that it can be misinterpreted if a woman asks a man to dinner or to go to a match or to play golf with her. Yet others, such as Sue, felt that spending time socialising with clients is not as important as spending time with family. Gladys and Victoria spoke for many of the interviewees in acknowledging that their lack of networking with the clients put them at a disadvantage compared with men, because it is just accepted that business is "done that way".

Well, I see women who are working are generally really busy and need to cut the crap and get down to the business. I sometimes sit in a meeting with clients and male colleagues and the clients are starting to get really fidgety and there's some bloke wittering on about how fantastic he is and suggesting getting tickets for the game but not actually getting into the nitty gritty and the detail of the business in hand. I think if you can pick up and read those signs 95% of women are like me – you don't want to muck around and you don't appreciate that carrying on and dancing around that the men do – this so-called networking. For me, I think it's just much more: "Here's what we've got to do, let's deal with it!"(Jo)

It is difficult inviting a male client to lunch or dinner without him misinterpreting the invitation, especially since I am single. (Maeve)

The male partners play golf with the clients. I have tried this myself but the children take precedence and I do not have the time to practise and play. If you have someone to yourself for five hours on the golf course, that gives you a nice advantage in relationship building. (Sue)

Because of the lack of networking skills with male clients, I think that women are worse than men at developing relationships with clients. (Gladys)

Not that I mind drinking, but I don't think women are as much into that male bonding thing over lots of pints. I would prefer to go to a concert or see a play. But it's hard to network with clients in a darkened theatre. (Victoria)

Belonging to a women's network

Thirdly, they saw networking as a mechanism for bringing together other elite women and forming a women's support group or network. There are moves, described by Sue, within the firms to support a women's network. These initiatives are having mixed success. There is some resistance, not from male colleagues, but from women staff members, as described by Colleen (see below). The dilemma of not wanting to belong to a women's group, but yet not being fully accepted in the men's network was explained well by Betty and by Vivienne.

One of the tax female partners that I was talking to used to say that in New York the female partners used to get together and have dialogues about some of the issues and things like that, sort of network amongst themselves. Now the firm is sponsoring a network of women partners and we will see how that works. (Sue)

I'm not a fantastic networker, but I work hard at it. I created my own opportunities and found ways to get lots of the firm's money to support a lot of women's networking things but I got no support from the women. (Colleen)

A women's network would be great, I think. But we don't want to be seen as a knitting circle, and so, I guess, we avoid anything formal. It is hard being a minority no matter how nice the men are. You see a big room full of male partners and one other woman: you want to gravitate across towards her but you don't want to set up a knitting circle. I don't enjoy networking with clients and lunching with them. For me it is a huge strain to have to go and sit and eat with people I don't really like. (Betty)

We work in a very 'blokey' environment. I am pretty blokey myself and I enjoy a pint and discussing sports, but sometimes the men are a bit uncomfortable in my presence even though I am joining in. (Vivienne)

Life-Work Balance

Life-work Balance (LWB) was seen as an obstacle the women had to overcome. Discussion on LWB focussed largely on balancing time at work with time for their children. Interviewees saw the major LWB issue for them as being the decisions about whether and when to have children, and how many children to have. As was shown in Table 4.3 in Chapter Four, the interviewees had a spread of children ranging from none to four, although 45% of them had no children and only 2% had four. Their reflection on the place of children in their lives was varied, but the following predominating themes emerged.

Decision to have children

The interviewees had different stories to tell relating to having children. However, there was a high proportion, including Rachel and Rose, who had deferred having children to progress their careers to the point, described by Karina, where they were "established". The wistful comment made by Maeve (see below) indicates the problem that can be associated with waiting for the career window to open sufficiently at the same time as the biological window is closing. Others had decided, like Ann and Victoria, not to have children in order to concentrate on their careers. Brenda indicated that this decision arose from her fear that she could not do justice to a motherhood role. Such decision-making is never easy and the kind of soul-searching that women experience was described well by Catherine.

> I hadn't started a family although we'd thought about it and talked about it and we just weren't ready for it even though I was getting older. We actually planned to start a family around about when I was 30 and then 32 and then 34 and we just sort of kept changing. But I figured it was easier to get to partnership without having a family. I think that it can slow women down on their track to partnership ... I think we're trying to do something about it within our organisation now, but when I went on maternity leave, our policy was three month's leave which I think is far too short and I wanted to extend my leave the first time, and the perception by some partners was that I wasn't committed because I put my family and myself ahead of the firm. And that hurt a lot because, you know, I'm very committed to the firm. (Rachel)

> We haven't got any children yet and we do intend to have a family. And I know that once we do that there's a whole lot of issues about how we're going to be able to cope. Rightly or wrongly I am of the belief that once we have children, that one of us is going to have to step back in terms of our career and I think it's likely to be me ... We've talked about this a lot and my husband doesn't have strong views. In fact, both of us are fighting to be the one to stay at home, really! (Rose)

Yes, that is another issue that makes me a little bit different, and probably my story would have been completely different and I may not be sitting here today if I had had my children at 32 or 33, which I guess is a more typical profile of somebody who is trying to be admitted. I had my children when I was 39 and 40, so I was six or seven years as partner, I had established myself and had good standing within the partnership, I didn't really have to prove myself, so therefore there was a lot of goodwill towards my going off and having my maternity leave and so forth. (Karina)

We haven't had children although we are trying, and we are having a bit of difficulty, I mean, I'm over 40 now, so that doesn't add to the ability to conceive, but we are still hopeful. (Maeve)

I could not have had the career to partnership with children. When we married, we had to decide then whether to have children or not, but I wanted to have a career and to earn good salary. So we didn't have a child. Now at this age, when it is too late, I have moments of regret. (Ann)

It's a bit different for me as I have no children. I just couldn't have had children and got myself up to partnership. I realized that I would always be lagging behind because of children, so we made the decision to press on with the target of partnership; I think I would like to have children eventually. I am only 37 now but know I shouldn't leave it too long. (Victoria)

I had decided not to have children. It's really impossible to be with them and do this job you know. The time for breast-feeding them and being with them when they take their first steps and anything more than just auditing and test checking their progress is just not possible! (Brenda)

The one thing I will be honest about, though and I don't talk about often because I wouldn't want to discourage talented women here, is that I grew up with an at-home Mum and I think I had a fantastic upbringing and if I did have children ... my initial thought is I'd want to do the same. I've watched women come back after three or six months, leaving the child with a nanny. I just don't think I'd want to do it; maybe I'd have to do it. I really don't know because I've never found myself in a situation of being pregnant and having to think it through. But I guess that's the piece about children whether I could have this job as well. I've never felt so strongly that I had to have children but I love kids, really love kids and now, I wonder – I don't know. (Catherine)

They had mixed experience of their male partners' attitudes, varying from the kind of support experienced by Norma and Aisling (see below) to the kind of umbrage described by Rachel and Trudy. The reaction described by Trudy and the sense of almost guilt at being pregnant as a partner, described by Maureen, supports the belief expressed by the focus group of the antipathy of the male partners to repeated maternity leave.

I have a child, a two and a half year old little boy. That was an amazing experience having him. I got a lot of support from the organisation which was fantastic. I'd only been a partner 18 months when I fell pregnant and it was amazing, "Well right, we'll do this, we'll cover there, come back whenever you want." That made me feel a hell of a lot of loyalty to the organisation. They were so excited because I was the first female partner to have a baby and I was very taken aback and surprised at how much support I really did have. (Norma)

I fell pregnant and I was about 24 weeks pregnant and I lost my baby and had a miscarriage and had a really, really tough time. It was just shocking. But the partners were just so supportive. The partners said: "Look take however much time you need. Don't worry about your work, we'll get it all sorted out, just look after yourself", which I felt extremely reassuring and at that time when your hormones are raging you feel like absolute shit. They were very, very supportive. So I thought yeah, I'll go again and see if I can ... you know, because we were very keen to start a family. So I fell pregnant again and everything was fine and I had a healthy little baby girl, which was wonderful. (Aisling)

So it just happened to work out that I got pregnant my first year as partner and there were two other women in the same boat and I remember some male partner made a comment: "Oh, we all know how the women partners celebrated getting made a partner!", because we were really all having babies. (Trudy)

I went for partnership and went through all the processes and after I had my interview I actually found out that I was pregnant. The announcement was due in three months and I really agonised around "My God, now should I tell people or what?". And I thought: "No. Why should it matter? It doesn't make any difference." And they were supposed to announce the partnership but it kept being delayed and I couldn't delay telling people that I was pregnant because I was just getting bigger. But I definitely felt that I should keep it quiet until the final announcement. (Maureen)

Hours of work

Interviewees acknowledged that they had to work very long hours to be considered for partnership, although they also talked about how much they enjoyed the hard work. They acknowledged that managing the punishing hours with children was more difficult than being childless.

I always believe that full-time is a very wide continuum. I always worked at the far end of it – the long end of it – too many hours. (Colleen)

I was lucky to choose a profession that is constantly intellectually challenging. I've never really been bored with what I do at work and sometimes I feel like it's too intellectually challenging and occasionally I'd like to do the same thing day after day but generally it's been something that inspires you to go to work. And it's quite exciting to be doing transactions; it's exciting to be doing things that are really making you think hard. (Jo)

I think the reasons I stayed at [name of Firm] really are people, opportunities and challenges and all of those things have held true from day one. (Maureen)

I love what I do, I love working with clients, I love the technical side, I love the fact that in essence we are still in academia, because you have to continue to study even though you are in a work environment, particularly with tax, they keep changing it every year, if not twice a year. (Maeve)

The hours are tough but I love it although I really couldn't have done these hours with children. (Victoria)

The twin rewards of enjoying the work and the high income appear to be significant for this group of women. So, although the hours were gruelling and the commitment to the firm and to the clients was intense, it appeared to be more than compensated for by the technical and intellectual challenge of the job, the enjoyment of working with interesting people and, in particular, the significant income. It is unlikely that they are different from the male partners in this regard, but they may be different from the women who quit or flee the profession.

People say you must love your career. Yeah I do, but if they didn't pay me I wouldn't do it! That is the test. If they said to me tomorrow, we know you love being a partner, but we are not giving you as much money any more, is that OK? No it's not! (Gillian)

People say that the money is very important. Yeah the money is great, it is fantastic and there are very few jobs that pay so well... But at the same time could you stay here if you were miserable? I don't think so. (Daisy)

These women had reconciled themselves to the necessity of working long hours. They acknowledged that the income gave them the financial freedom to pay for the domestic support necessary to maintain their homes and to rear their children.

I don't have children, but even if I had children now I think it wouldn't make such a difference, because we have enough money. If you can pay good money for childcare, that makes life much easier. Whereas if you have children when you are more junior, it is horrendous. You don't have the money to put in place a structure around childcare. That means that you are always struggling and worried about them. (Mary)

You know I think what I was earning as a senior manager before I became a partner was enough for me in a financial sense. It wasn't enough from an ego sense but from a financial sense it was. But I've got friends, women who are at home looking after their kids and I couldn't even imagine having to rely on my husband to hand me out money. You know even if I had control over it, if somebody else has earned it, I just couldn't do that. (Jo)

We like the money. It makes my life a little bit easier. I have full-time childcare, a nanny effectively, from 8 am to 6.30 pm. I'm only on my second nanny ever, because I can afford to pay her very well. I wouldn't if I was earning a smaller income. I pay her a substantial amount of money. I have a cleaner, which I couldn't otherwise afford. I have my clothes ironed. We do Internet shopping and you don't spend time looking at what you are paying. I go on holidays at the last moment because I don't have time to plan them. So because we earn good money, the money facilitates life outside of work. (Gladys)

I'm financially independent, totally independent of my husband, and I really enjoy that. So, if God forbid, something ever happens to him, I wouldn't have to change my standard of living, which is important to me. I think perhaps it's like with anything: the more you have of the good thing, the more you want of it, so my earnings have increased dramatically over the last couple of years, and I certainly would not want to forego it. I enjoy it. I enjoy spending. I enjoy beautiful things, and a beautiful home, and I guess I probably would describe myself as being materialistic, and I think I've probably become worse over the years. (Hannah)

I enjoy the money and what it can bring. The money gave me independence from my husband which was very important, especially over the divorce period. (Vivienne)

However, there were downsides, as described by Linda, who worried that her children had too comfortable a lifestyle, and for Miriam, who described how her high income was used against her in financial negotiations surrounding divorce.

In a strange kind of way it's one of the things I miss: not having something to strive for. We do have a good income. It's one of the things I worry about with my kids, one of the reasons I would be pretty intent on keeping the lifestyle reasonably modest, because I don't want my children to think there is money coming out their ears, I don't think it's a particularly good thing. (Linda)

So he just left me and then the money fight happened. I felt incredibly attacked and because I had such a good income, I was harassed for half my wealth. He wanted to take half our home where I'd paid for it. My strong financial situation was a hammer to attack me with. (Miriam)

WHAT STRATEGIES DID THEY EMPLOY TO PROGRESS?

As I listened to the women and when I analysed the transcripts of their interviews, some common stratagems emerged that they used to achieve partnership, in addition to the normal gender non-specific tactics. They can be grouped under the following headings:

- acceptance of the 'partnership track';
- putting in place support mechanisms (being married, stress management techniques, good childcare); and
- spending time overseas.

Acceptance of the partnership track

Of course, in common with male candidates, the women had to be intelligent, good with clients, problem-solvers, and so on. They referred to the 'partnership track' as a process almost outside of their immediate control. They were independent, powerful women, but the track was described (e.g. by Delia, Deirdre and Priscilla) as having a force of its own. The track, as Mary explained, is structured and clearly understood within the firms. Candidates are identified and mentored towards partnership. Getting onto this track is a combination of strategic positioning by the candidate, but mostly identification of the candidate as 'partnership material' by the firm. The candidate for partnership has to engage with the process and step up to the mark with the performance indicators demanded. As long as the candidate works hard and continues to achieve good performance reviews, he or she is guided and given appropriate further indicators along the way.

The majority of the interviewees stepped onto the Big Four career path early in their professional lives and Sarah (see below) was characteristic of this. In some cases, especially where their degree was non-business, the careers started in areas such as banking and law. Some interviewees moved, soon after qualifying, from one Big Four firm (or Big Six or Eight as they then were) to another. However, mostly they committed themselves early on in their careers to the firm that subsequently elected them to partnership and did not move within the Big Four.

Once they entered the partnership track they understood and accepted that dedicated commitment was necessary to advance to partnership. Many felt that, unlike their male peers, they did not plan their careers themselves and that the management of their career paths appeared to be dictated by the tried and tested model of progression to partnership – the partnership track – which is similar for all the Big Four firms. So, although they spoke of their need to be in control of their technical and professional lives, there was little evidence of them taking control of their career path. The firm's partnership track was laid out for them by others and they had to conform to the objectives set for them. As described by Norma (see below) they accepted its strictures although they, unlike their male colleagues, baulked at the unspoken need to self-market or 'blow their own trumpet'.

I didn't like the firm, I didn't like [name of Big Four firm] at all. It was extremely competitive, very aggressive, very successful, very emphasizing success. Nobody would support each other. There was no teamwork, and not good values as far as I was concerned, so, I moved to [name of another Big Four firm] when I qualified, and I've been here ever since. (Sarah)

Recognising the game of self-promotion doesn't come naturally, I don't think, to most women. For some it does, some are really, really good at it and really enjoy it, but most women are like me. I don't like it, I don't like singing from my song book about myself. But people need to know, you need to get recognition. I guess I don't like it up to a point but if I can see other people being recognised when I'm not being recognised then that's when I really get into that game because it's just not fair. (Norma)

The ladder is very clear and well-structured and I was without doubt interested in the income and the security that goes with partnership. (Mary)

I spent a week with my sister in the last couple of weeks and we were talking about how we ended up where we did and we just hadn't a clue, I had no career plan at all. (Delia)

You have to be spotted by the partners. It was partners' view of the potential that mattered. I had to have a network of people whom I had worked with over the years and had seen me in all sorts of environments and tough situations. When you are being made a partner, I think there is an element that you should be focussing only on the partnership. You were expected to focus on your career and not on getting married and having children. It is not as overt as that, but I think, looking back on it now, I did unconsciously think that this is my career and I am going to really work on this for the next four or five years. That did happen. (Daisy)

I never really focused at any stage on the fact that I wanted to be a partner. I never specifically set that out as my ultimate goal. My goals were always more immediate, whenever I had an appraisal my goals were more short-term than long-term. (Deirdre)

I went for partnership in that year and got partnership. I don't think I had even stopped to think about what I was doing. I was just on one track, I focussed on the journey, not the destination and I worked huge hours. (Priscilla)

One of the senior partners who I work with said to me, "What would you like to do in the futures?" And I think he obviously wanted me to stay here. I think he was probably saying to me: 'Do you want to become a partner?' At that stage in my career I guess I just never in a million years imagined that I would have it in me that I had the skills to become a partner. I probably thought that all the way until I became a partner. (Maureen)

Being made partner was described as very exciting. It was characterised as a tidal wave of great external force. It was as if they, rowing their boats, had to travel in the direction the wave was taking them. So long as they paddled strongly and wisely in the direction dictated by the wave, they stayed afloat, although many capsized. Eventually, the wave landed them on the golden, palm-fringed beach of partnership and retreated to collect the next cohort. On the beach, the external force had ended and somehow they were expected to take control of their own progress. Once this realisation of their new role dawned and of their changed status and control, the women showed little evidence of sharp career management. They spoke of the freedom their new role gave them to organise their own lives and to select the niche areas suited to their competencies. However, there appeared to be no structured career management for partners to advise or guide them. In selecting their own post-partnership pathways, many of the women were assumed to want to gravitate towards the human resource and people management area of the partnership. However, they expressed a sense of unease and of feeling poorly equipped to fill those roles. They also felt reluctant to pursue partnership leadership roles. Miriam described having to look around for herself to find a post-partnership niche and Brenda spoke of staying in the comfort zone she had developed for herself.

> I think up until that time [election to partnership] I'd had regular changes in my career. I'd sort of been studying and then gone to UK, come back, manager, group manager, partner and obviously all of those were changes. I enjoyed the work most of the time but in retrospect there wasn't a lot of change after I became partner. And I tended to work on similar clients and maybe that was partly me. I enjoyed the clients that I was working on and I didn't sort of agitate to shift onto other clients and I wasn't interested in getting into practice leadership roles in the firm – like the policy committee or being managing partner – which some other people did. I was more interested in dealing with the clients and being involved in that sort of work so I stayed put. (Brenda)

> I'm just not the sort of person who's ever planned and plotted my career. You'll probably meet some that are, each step of it. I see myself more as a wave. I'm on a wave – not very good about talking about really clear goals, I'm on a wave and I will generally go the right direction and I'm getting there. But I find that far more interesting than calculating each stage and ticking off each stage because

sometimes the diversions along the way are riches, either learnings or moments you have with people. So here I am going through my normal: "Gosh I'm a partner, oh my God how that's different, oh we're not in the same business anymore and nobody is really talking to me about it." That was a huge overwhelming period. But I landed on my feet, found a spot in the audit group where I could do what I do. And from that point I've learned and I tell a lot of people here: "Learn, hear what the firm's doing with strategy, go and hear those power point presentations from the CEO and ask yourself where you fit in this. Because if you start to feel in a place like this that you don't fit anymore, you can't see your own fit, strategic fit, value fit, you're going to be in big trouble. (Miriam)

I had no career path. I had no idea where I was going to proceed to after being made partner. (Ann)

Why am I still here? I'm not sure at the moment, it's a tough existence and in some ways it's been much easier since I've been a partner because I'm more definite in what I will do and what I won't do. I think it would be too strong to say that I am beginning to look at my future although I know I – we, all of us partners should spend more time thinking of our own career plans. It is more that I am looking at my present and my current life–work balance. (Loretta)

The interviewees all referred to a number of support mechanisms that they put in place to sustain themselves in their appointment to partnership. These included being married, prioritising demands on their time, stress management strategies and childcare (where they had children).

Being married

Being married was seen by many interviewees as important in pursuing an elite career, both (as explained by Orna) because it made relationships with male mentors and clients more comfortable and because (as noted by Karina) not being 'on the scene' meant that they were not distracted from the pursuit of a career. Only 23% of the interviewees were single and their mean age was 39 years.

You have to be very careful when you are seeking out a mentor as a woman (because the mentors will nearly all be men). You don't want to give out any wrong signals and so that's why it's easier when you have a husband and everyone knows that. (Orna)

I am single and that presents difficulties in terms of how I am viewed and also just the lack of support. (Fionnuala)

It is nearly the best position to be in from a career perspective probably to be married with no children. You don't have to struggle to devote time to 'being on the scene' – you know – your social life and meeting guys, which is time-consuming and you don't have the tie of kids. If you are married with no children or in a relationship with no children, life is very comfortable and you have plenty of time for yourself and your partner and your work. (Karina)

The married interviewees (like Aisling) saw the support of their spouse as very important to their capacity to progress their careers. However, where spouses had demanding careers as well there were considerable strains to contend with. Where the marriage had difficulties, the stress of partnership seemed to make matters worse. Many interviewees accepted (as Michelle typically did) that they did not spend enough time on their relationship with their spouses and although they acknowledged the support and understanding of their husbands, it appeared that their relationships were severely tested.

Fair enough I am a partner, but at a huge personal cost to my marriage. I actually don't think the two are totally related. There are other things as well. But I don't think that I could have been a partner without the cost to my marriage. (Delia)

My husband is very, very helpful and he's great. You know he helps as much as he can but he works full-time and he works Saturdays and he works very often late at night you know ten, eleven o'clock at night too. (Aisling)

What was happening was we were rotating. We never saw each other: work on a Saturday and work on a Sunday. He kept saying he would give up and I didn't really believe him and one day I came home and [he] said he had quit and I went "Oh my God!". I was delighted for a while, but it was difficult because men don't really quit their jobs. We looked at a number of things and I discovered that the only way a man can go back to work is to go back full-time. It was difficult socially and, luckily, we kept our child minder at the same time. (Susan)

I acknowledged that I do not devote enough time to [name of husband]. I feel there is a disproportionate support network with me taking more than I give to him. He is a teacher and is often inflexible about time to pick up the kids and that can be a problem. I do have to admit that he is a more committed parent than I am – and that's tough, that's tough. (Michelle)

I think whenever you have both parties working I think you're always going to find there is a lack of time. I think it's important for you to really sit down and have some quality time together because you're both under so much pressure at work. When you've been at work all day, sometimes it's actually a struggle whether you want to have a conversation with someone else at all. I think there are a lot of advantages as well because we both understand the sort of pressures. So we see that as a very good advantage and also we can bounce ideas off one another, we can talk through issues but the downside is that sometimes you do double the stress. If both of you are having a bad day then it's pretty hard. (Rose)

I am recently divorced and I think that the hours at work finally broke my marriage. I really became physically and mentally exhausted as a result of the stress and of the divorce. (Vivienne)

He was a great support. It took seven years for him to really understand but he was, and always is, my best friend. (Colleen)

I know that it is important to spend time on my relationship with my husband. It is imperative if the marriage is to survive. But I recognise that it is easier for me as I have no children. (Yvonne)

I have always believed that getting married early was good for career development, not least because it took you out of the market place and made working relationships in the heavily male dominated environment much easier. (Ann)

Prioritising demands

The women realised that their professional careers placed enormous demands on their time. This clearly meant that time was not available for other parts of their lives. They were conscious that, while they liked to think of themselves as superwomen – able to manage time for work, time for children, time for friends, time for their husbands and time for themselves, it just was not possible to fit everything in and they realised they had to prioritise. When each reflected on her list of priorities, it was very common for the child/children to come first, the job to come next, time for herself then, and for her husband to come last.

> My priorities would be: my son and then the job – career – then probably me and then [name of husband]. Yeah – he probably comes after me – unfortunately. But I think we're realising that I earn a lot of money. I would like to think that I'd put him a little bit before me, but I think, in reality, I probably don't. (Norma)

> I love my children to death and they're the most important thing in my life. So they are the most important before my job. I have very little time for myself and probably even less for [name of husband]. (Sue)

Stress management strategies

Interviewees referred consistently to the stressful nature of their lives. In one or two cases, they appeared to be just about hanging on and managing the stress, and many referred to the increasingly stressful nature of the professional role in the extant economic and regulatory circumstances. They referred to strategies such as a healthy lifestyle, diet and exercise as ways of managing this significant factor. However, in many cases, they admitted that they found it hard to make time to fit them in, and there were several mentions of being conscious of relying on a 'glass of wine' to relax when they would have been better off going for a run. It was a common response to identify (as Deirdre did) the strategy of keeping on top of their workload as a successful means of keeping stress at bay. Many referred to additional stress associated with maternity leave, and many took less than the statutory period, either because they felt under pressure from their partners or because they wanted to get back to work.

Really the only way I've dealt with stress and difficult issues is just to keep at it and just to work hard to get things done and not let them pile up. I try to be organised so that I pre-empt things or get things started early. (Deirdre)

It is a stressful job and, no doubt about it, clients can be demanding. (Delia)

I felt very stressed when I watched some of my peers who had children and some of them were working three days a week and they were getting 60% profit share. But I was working far, far more hours than they were. They were probably only working 40% of the hours I did and yet they got 60% profit share. I found that very stressful and it was a period of resentment because I was always there and was treated like the old reliable. (Katy)

I found the 4 or 5 weeks I was off on maternity leave very difficult, because I wasn't used to being off and I was used to going home late in the evening. When I went back to work, that is where the tension started to build, I would have been used to coming home at 10 or 11 at night and all of a sudden I had to go home two nights per week with my husband and I couldn't leave for work until 8 am in the morning. So I found that quite difficult and quite stressful and I wasn't used to it, I wasn't used to having to go home on a Friday evening. That I found very difficult. (Susan)

I've been trying to be a super woman for the last 18 months and I must admit I think I'm failing quite badly. I feel that I'm not spending enough time with my children and at the same time I feel that you know I could spend more time at work. I mean I could work 24 hours a day seven days a week if I wanted to because we have just been so busy. There's been a lot of changes in regulation, in international financial reporting standards that apply. The clients are becoming a lot more demanding. The deadlines are becoming tighter, it's just not the way we did business 10 years ago, it's just becoming a lot more cut-throat, a lot more focused, a lot more on edge. (Aisling)

I was very unfit. I was much heavier than I am now. I didn't look after myself for 4–5 years and then I made very conscious efforts to be fit and look after myself and I very much do that now. I try to walk three times a week. (Daisy)

I play sport that makes me feel good. We eat reasonably healthily now. We drink too much alcohol according to my health assessment. (Norma)

I could do a better job of caring for my health. I probably don't sleep as much as I should, although I've always been able to function on limited sleep. And I eat healthy food, and I think I'm active because I've two little boys I have to chase around after, but I'll be 40 this year and I realise that I really need to be much more disciplined about exercise. I've been lucky, in general I have really good health, it hasn't been something where I've had to worry. (Trudy)

I am quite healthy, and I've always enjoyed eating healthy food so I don't really worry that way, but I don't exercise enough and I do drink too much wine, definitely, every night. (Sarah)

Childcare

Having children was clearly a wonderful experience for the majority of the interviewees who were mothers. However, Maureen's and Sue's responses reflected the sense of guilt that some of them experienced at leaving their children in the hands of others. They also spoke of how they rationalised their actions in order to ameliorate that guilt.

Although, in talking of their priorities, their children came before their careers, many spoke about putting in place appropriate supports that would allow them to pursue their careers at a very high level, safe in the knowledge that they had put in place the best childcare money could buy. (Aisling typified this view – see below.) Even those who did not have children, like Daisy, referred to the need for strong supports, were they ever to have them. A strongly recurring theme was the organisation necessary to ensure that they have "quality time with the kids", although Linda, who had successfully negotiated a part-time partnership, expressed the contrary view that 'quantity time' is better.

I don't have children, but if I ever did I would put in place the mechanism to have someone look after them. I would make sure that I lived very close to town, not spending time commuting. I would have lots of infrastructure in place and that is how I would do it, but I wouldn't give up work. (Daisy)

I've got a great Nanny and I've got very supportive parents, so I've got a pretty good network of people that can help and look after the kids. (Aisling)

I got used to the idea that childcare is a normal thing. I've, over the years, had a lot of guilt trips in terms of "Will the children love the carer more than me?" But what I've learnt – and you don't know this before you have kids – is that the children think you're fantastic. And when I walk in at night they come racing towards me and they bowl me over and they make me feel so good and you just realise that nothing is going to take away the bond you have. (Maureen)

I had my kids when I was in my early thirties. You know that was a decision that I went back and forth on. When was the right time? You can agonise, I want to have this amount of money saved, I want to live in this sized house or whatever, there's no right time. Number one you have to be ready. But it took us a long time. For three years we tried. Ideally after five years of marriage I would have liked to have a child so it took us an extra three years. But it happened, it worked, and I think the timing was good. Sometimes I wonder whether I might have some more energy if I'd had them when I was younger, but I don't know. I still worry about whether they are getting less from me than if I stayed at home full-time but we get them into lots of things. Even just the things that they're involved in, we try to have diverse activities. So we have our oldest in a religious school for an hour and a half one day a week. He's in swimming lessons, he's played soccer a couple of seasons, now he's chosen baseball, you know, he got tired of soccer. So we try to do different things to get exercise, to stimulate the mind, he's not bored. (Sue)

What was the point of having kids if you don't spend time with them? I didn't care what the rest of the world thought about it. I wanted to get home, and the one thing I feel very strongly about is turning up regularly. To hell with quality time. I think a lot of it is just being there for quantity time – being there everyday, for as long as you can manage to be there. It's the only way you will have any idea of what is going on. (Linda)

Spending time overseas

Many of the interviewees referred to the opportunities for travel within their firms and for getting overseas experience. They saw this as an important element of their campaign for partnership. A good external experience on their CV was seen as a significant delineator of success.

[The firm] approached me and asked if I would be interested in going on a strategic career development programme which is a programme for the people they believe have long-term potential and they'd like to retain in the firm. (Katy)

RESISTANCE TO FLIGHT

One of the major issues for the accountancy firms is the higher proportion of women who 'quit', even though they may be identified as partnership material. In assessing the experience of the interviewees to determine how they resisted the pattern of women quitting the profession in greater proportions than men, and why they remain as partners, some features emerged that might be classified as further predictors of success for them. Those features were:

- controlling the temporal boundaries as the 'boss';
- considering part-time working;
- identifying a partnership role for themselves; and
- avoiding engagement with office politics.

Control of the temporal boundaries as the 'Boss'

As discussed above, the interviewees referred to an inactive approach to the management of their careers once they had achieved partnership. They employed strategies to manage their post-partnership career by exercising more control of their temporal boundaries.

They knew that, in order to achieve partnership, it was imperative to work very long hours, including working weekends, early mornings and late nights. Mary and Trudy described the hours expected and, in extreme cases, such as those described by Melanie, the volume of work led to a sense of loss of control and high stress levels. They accepted this external setting of their temporal boundaries while they were striving for partnership. However, once they were elected to partnership, they saw possibilities of taking back control of their temporal boundaries and of resetting them to suit themselves by working hours, albeit still long hours, in a way that accommodated their lives better. Belinda, Linda and Delia described how this happened. Rachel referred to the oft-repeated collaboration – almost collusion – with their secretaries, in organising her diary to accommodate other commitments. In some cases, this included considering working part-time. This was possible by virtue of 'being the boss'.

Well, I am at my desk at half seven most mornings and I would rarely leave before 8 at night. I usually have work to take home and generally work over the weekend as well. I have some good friends who drag me off for dinner or a show occasionally, but I know that my hours are manic and that I'll have to curtail them but I just enjoy the work. (Mary)

I usually bring my kids to school, so I don't tend to come in early. I was considered a bit of a joke coming in late every morning at 9 o'clock. But then I worked all day. I used to leave in time to hear the 9 o'clock news, then I moved nearer to the office and, ironically, I never heard the news again. I was never home in time for it. Most partners would do minimum 500 hours overtime a year. (Belinda)

Here I was in a business that was expanding greatly. I just couldn't keep going. I was working manic hours. You hear about these things happening, but you never envisaged it happening to you and I didn't know what was happening, it was more worrying than having cancer, because I couldn't get myself under control. (Melanie)

When I worked at [name of firm] I worked very, very hard. It was very demanding, I worked all the time. You had to work weekends you had to work late at night and it wasn't like you had a lot of autonomy when you are not a partner. Even if you had all your work done, if everyone in your group was there, you were there. It was: "Let's all man the ship and gather around the totem pole." (Trudy)

Now I try (except in busy season) not to come into the office at the weekend. I am the exception to that – everyone else is here. I have to do the shopping on Saturday morning. I actually like to do the shopping myself and know what is going on and what is being eaten in the house. The staff will say it's all right for you, you are the partner. I think as a partner you are more able to dictate your own terms and if I have to go, I go. (Belinda)

It's easier being a partner than it is being a senior manager, much easier, because you have control over your life. It's hard to get rid of you. It is hard for anyone to come in and start picking apart what you have done. This is my office. I decide what I am going to do from one end of the day to the other. It's great. (Linda)

I remember one year here it was my birthday and I was working on Saturday on my birthday. I was in here with a student and a consultant and supervisor working with me and I remember saying that it's my birthday and the student said: "At least you have a choice whether you come in on a Saturday and your birthday. I am only here because you want me here. I'd prefer to be out playing hockey!" I think being a partner gives me enormous flexibility, I am my own boss. I can come and go when I want. Nobody asks me where I am or when I will be in or leave. This gives me the flexibility to work at home, or, obviously subject to client restraints, I might take a half day or something and do the work tonight or tomorrow night instead. (Delia)

When I was made a partner my life was much easier than when I was manager, because in a way you are your own master and you are responsible for yourself, within a firm you are not answerable to anybody. A partner said to me once about 15 years ago, 'being a partner is like having your own business within 60 little businesses'. I find it much easier to do it my way and you don't have to balance all these other people screaming for your time and wanting you to do all these different things. (Daisy)

I think the power is what keeps me there, you don't have somebody telling you what to do. Any of the stress in your work environment is self induced; you actually are responsible for your own day to day activity. It is great, so if I decide not to come in until 9.30 am that is fine. I can go home at 4 pm if I need to. I can go to the children's school play without being accountable to anyone else. (Susan)

My secretary assists me in doing that, so we just block time out of my diary so people can't contact me. So there's flexibility in being a partner that you don't have in being an employee and I just don't think employees are aware that partners take that flexibility because we don't talk about it, we don't promote it, we just do it. (Rachel)

Working part-time

Four of the interviewees were working or had worked part-time as partners. There was mixed reaction to that experience. While their male partners seemed supportive, they experienced an undercurrent of resistance. Of the four, two felt it was working well (although one had only just started); one reported resistance and the fourth found that she had been gradually sucked into working a full work load (including being contacted on her days at home) even thought she was only paid 60% profit share. She went back to full-time working. Other partners spoke of considering part-time working, but felt that it would not be acceptable. Some women, who were approaching retirement, felt that it would be a good way of easing out of the partnership, although none had done anything to pursue the idea. Delia also pointed out that part-time partnership, insofar as it was available at all, was assumed to be of interest only to women with children. These views provided some confirmation of the hostility expressed by the male partners in the focus group to part-time partnerships.

People make judgements that things can't work without even knowing whether they can work. As a female and as a working mother that's one thing that I've really learnt over the last four years. I was told that part-time partners wouldn't work. So when I had my first child I came back three days a week for three months and then four days a week for eighteen months but I was told it wouldn't work. And then, I was put under pressure to come back full-time. The partners said it wasn't working, but my team and staff said that I was available and that it was fine. So the only people who thought this didn't work were the partners and I think that's because they're not in the same space and they don't think the same way and it's such a radical thing for them to accept that anybody could work part-time let alone a women working part-time. (Rachel)

I decided I would go three days a week. So I had my two children and it's been almost six years now that I've worked three days a week, and I have to say it's worked incredibly well. And I think part of it is I have this sort of feeling like my kids are really important to me and this is what I'm willing to do. And if it's not acceptable to the firm or the people around me that's fine, but this is what I have to offer. And I don't have more than this. (Trudy)

Part time? Well, I was talking to one of the male partners who is my age when the part-time policy was introduced, I said "I might apply for that", and he said: "You don't have any children", and I said: "Where does it say that you have to have children." Apparently some of the older partners think that it is only for women with children and that they should restrict the number working part time. They are happy to bend over backwards for staff, why we wouldn't do it for the partners is beyond me. (Delia)

Finding a partnership role

Much of the emphasis of the interviewees' reflections was on how they had succeeded in making it to partnership and how they were managing the very demanding life style they had now. They had not planned how their future careers as partners would develop and progress, although many talked of finding a niche for themselves. Hannah represented the sentiments of many who said that it had been assumed that they would be interested in becoming the Human Resources (HR) partner and the partner with counselling responsibility, because they were women. Some, like Ann, were comfortable with that assumption, but others like Hannah lamented the lack of career planning for partners and specific training for the HR and counselling roles they found themselves undertaking. Fionnuala explained well the resistance that some of the interviewees felt when it was assumed they would take on the HR roles, owing to the non-chargeable nature of the work. Older partners, like Gillian and Niamh, were giving some thought to retirement planning, although nothing structured emerged and, again, the lack of post-partnership career planning within the firms was evident.

There is huge subjectivity in the profit sharing and you have to work unrealistically hard to get over 100% share. Women partners are expected to do a lot of the HR work, but this kind of unbillable time is difficult when it comes to sharing the profit. (Fionnuala)

The women partners are expected to look after the HR side more than the male partners. But we get absolutely no training in it. I am an accountant and yet I am expected to handle difficult personal problems for staff just because I am a woman. (Hannah)

I think I interact well with staff and colleagues – probably better than my male partners. A lot of people would use me either as a sounding board or as a lightning rod just to work through issues together, both because I am a woman and because I am at the stage of my career where I am not going anywhere, I am not a threat to other people. (Ann)

We need, as a firm, to have a more structured approach to partners as they near the end of their careers. There should be more planning and more phasing and more use of the knowledge. I wonder why some of them are actually still here? There are a number of them [who] came in at 21 and are still here 30 odd years later, never having left the firm. I think I am a sad bastard but they are worse. I am one of the first women coming to the end of a partnership career and we need to think about our descent down the slippery pole. I think we can retire early at 55 and I think I will go. One of the reasons I would leave is that I am a little bit burnt out. (Gillian)

I don't think I will be here when I am 65, we have an early retirement programme and people tend to leave when they are 55. You are not thrown out, but I am already starting to feel that my clients are younger than me. (Delia)

My retirement age is 58 anyway but you know sometimes you wonder if one of the ways of them doing it to you is to slowly reduce your profit share so that you will get the message that it's uneconomic for you to stay. I remember being made a partner and I thought, "Well what's next, you know, what else is left?" I will be pushed out of here but I am concerned to have something to move on to. I don't have children to spend time with and I will never have grandchildren, which I sometimes regret. (Niamh)

Well of course in the track to partnership, it was tight and well planned and almost planned for me by the firm's career routing, but now, well yes, to be frank, I don't really have time to think too much about my own future, although I guess ... that's probably another day's work. (Collette)

I'm almost at the end of my time, retire in a few years time, I want to retire at 55, but, I've been told that I can stay until 60, so, I'll try work my way out slowly – but no real plans. (Betty)

I can sit and I can think, maybe I should be doing something else, maybe I would like to try something else, then I think what else would I do, what else can I do actually, sounds terrible but, what else would I do, and what else would I like to do? And I've often thought of lecturing and things like that, and then I sit down and I think, let me really consider the detail, let me imagine what I would do each day and I don't know. If I sit down and I actually think about my daily activity, I actually enjoy my daily activity, I drive to work and I'm happy and you know, I sit at my desk and I've got a beautiful view, you know, a wonderful environment, I work with amazing people, they are youngsters who challenge me. I'm obviously getting on a bit now, so the youngsters are challenging and they keep you on your toes, sometimes you feel gosh, it's really difficult, but that's why I enjoy that, and it's good for me, so, despite my thoughts that well maybe I should move, I wouldn't go to another big four firm because of loyalty to [name of firm], and obviously I've been brought up by them, I'm like their child you know, afterwards you are almost married to the firm. So, I look at it and I'm still here. (Maeve)

Office politics

Interviewees were *ad idem* against the possibility of engaging politically in the firm's leadership structures. They expressed the view that they and, in their observation, women in general, are not interested in such a role.

So, women are less likely to enjoy the whole office politics of going for a role in practice management once they become partners. They hate the politics, quite apart from the extra work. And it goes back to the fact that there is so much stress in the system right now, you know, accounting firms are getting sued all the time, audit jobs are blowing up. As I keep telling people, we can't be private investigators of our clients but that's what the market place expects. So it's just a very difficult environment. I noticed recent appointments to national positions in the firm and I said to the managing partner, 'Of all these 35 positions that you have slots for, whether it be partner in charge of an office, partner in charge of a practice like International, State, Local or whatever, I said, Do you realise that there's not one woman? Not one'. And he said, "You're right". The next day he appointed a woman in one of those key positions. (Fionnuala)

I'm not a politician though. I do try and get along with other people. I think it's very important for people to work well together and it bothers me when people don't get along, even though I know that that's impossible, but I try to be sort of a person that brings people together to the extent that I can, but I'm not a person who just says something because it's what someone wants to hear, I have to believe it. To be the Chairman of the firm, you have to be willing to make enemies and to live with that. I don't think that's me. (Catherine)

I would not see myself going for the CEO job. I would lose the direct contact with my staff and clients, which I love. You would be sort of isolated, and I don't really know would I want that. I'd love to be on their committee, you know, advising the CEO, but I don't know if I want to be the CEO. (Liz)

Summary

Chapters 4 and 5 described the outcomes of the preliminary studies and the interviews with the women partners. The main themes emerging were described. Chapter 6 pulls the findings of this research together and makes some recommendations for women partners, women candidates for partnership and for the firms themselves.

6

♦

CONCLUSIONS AND RECOMMENDATIONS

What Can we Learn from Our Elite Women?

Forty three women partners in Big Four Firms told us of their lives, their backgrounds, characteristics, career path and hopes, anxieties, successes and disappointments. They shared this information with us honestly and frankly. They made it clear that they did so in the hope that it would prove possible to extract some general themes that would help young women who aspire to achieve partnership; and that it might help their firms to strengthen the environment in which they will do business into the future. Hopefully, the exercise of reflecting on their own lives and pathways to date was useful to them as well. We can summarise the outcome of this research under these three perspectives, viz.:

- Women who aspire to partnership
- The current women partners
- The Big Four firms

Women Aspirants to Partnership

Women who are currently considering the possibility of an elite career in accountancy can consider what the voices of the women are saying to them. The lessons, from their experiences, seem to be that aspirants to partnership should:

Have the appropriate characteristics

To have a likelihood of achieving partnership, women should, in addition to having strong technical expertise and an excellent academic record, be competitive, independent, display self-confidence (even if they are full of self-doubt), blow their own trumpets (even if it goes against the grain) and be motivated by a challenging problem-solving job with high financial reward.

The evidence from this study suggests that the partnership culture in the Big Four firms is masculine. I would argue, based on that evidence, that, until there is a critical mass of people with feminine characteristics at the top of the firms, women displaying predominantly masculine characteristics are more likely to fit the profile. However, this is capable of change if the current women partners and the incoming women partners recognise the culture and agree to work together to change the environment so that genuine diversity is valued and rewarded. Women need to construct their own identity at the top of the accountancy profession. The male model is comfortable for people with predominantly masculine characteristics, but people with predominantly feminine characteristics (which does, of course, include some men) need to define and construct their own space. In order to do this, they need to be present in significant numbers. This means that there should be more women, creating their own space as a feminine space, building relationships in their own way and building a work pattern that aligns with their different leadership styles and different rhythms of life. While it would be good if men understood that this were happening, the spadework to effect the change must be done by women, working together. This could be helped by effective women's networks and discussion groups. Sadly, it would appear that the current attitude to the formation of such groups by women is one of suspicion.

Have the required background

For women aspirants, it is too late to change their background when they are at a stage to present for partnership. In general, this study shows that it does not matter what their parents did for a living or whether they had a trauma-free childhood or not. However, there was a clear preponderance of women partners who had attended a single-sex school, were good at mathematics, resisted any attempt at gender stereotyping and went on to third level to study a business-related degree. Although women aspirants cannot change these factors for themselves, awareness of these preferences may prove useful in breaking the mould. It may also prove interesting for gate-keepers to redirect their gaze towards women who, for example, went to a co-educational school, displayed language rather than mathematical prowess; or undertook third-level education in areas such as human resource management, psychology or social science.

This research indicates that women whose parents were supportive rather than pushy as they were growing up are more likely to achieve partnership. Again, this cannot be changed by current aspirants, but may be useful information for anyone who is considering parenthood.

Overcome the barriers and engage support strategies

The results of this study suggest that women aspirants should not think negatively about the barriers that women encounter in seeking elite positions in accountancy. Enjoying the work and being technically excellent are necessary prerequisites. Additionally, they must be willing to work the unsociable hours and give the commitment demanded. They must be willing to focus on the barriers as a challenge that can be overcome and engage in strategies that will support them in achieving partnership and, subsequently, in the role of partner. This may involve deciding against motherhood, restricting the size of their family or deferring motherhood until they are established as partners.

Identifying a powerful mentor is key to achieving partnership. This presents an obstacle for some women as there are not enough female mentors to offer them the three-stranded approach of role modelling, social support and career development that characterise good mentoring. The women participating in this study support the probability that aspirants are more likely to succeed if they seek out and develop a mentoring relationship with a male partner who will expose their work to other partners. This informal mentoring relationship appeared to work better than a formal mentoring relationship with an allocated mentor. This, of course, will involve networking with other partners and with a range of clients. The network is often a 'boys' club' and there is little evidence of any 'girls' network' at the top of the profession. Aspirants need to find a way that suits their life style, of engaging with the network, but, at the same time, being comfortable with their level of involvement in the more masculine activities (golf, sport, drinks after work etc.) that surround it. There may, indeed, be opportunities to be pioneers, to network with women clients and colleagues and to begin to construct a network that is supportive and productive to women.

Strategies that are used

Arising from this study, women aspirants would be advised to consider some strategies that appear to have been successful. First, the aspirant should carefully weigh up the cost in terms of time and commitment and balance it against the financial reward and status that attach to partnership. If, on considered reflection, the cost is outweighed by the benefit, she should actively seek to have herself considered for the partnership track. Consultation with a powerful mentor would be useful at this point. Even though the firm appoints a specific mentor or counselling partner, aspirants are advised to seek out informal mentor/s who seem to be a good fit for them.

Aspirants should devise an appropriate stress and health management plan for themselves. There are obvious dangers in entering the partnership track if the concomitant stress leads to ill-health.

A period of overseas or client assignment appears to be a useful strategy and aspirants would be advised to consider their options in this regard. This may involve deferring relationships and/or motherhood. Discussion with a good mentor would again prove beneficial in this decision.

The male environment, cross-gender mentoring, and socialising and networking with male colleagues and clients, can pose potential difficulties for women. The women participating in this study identified being married to a supportive spouse as a helpful stratagem. It freed up time to allow them to concentrate on their careers (i.e. time not spent meeting potential spouses); and meant that there could be no misinterpretation of invitations to clients, mentors and colleagues to conduct business in a social setting. However, the elite women were conscious that they did not have enough time to spend on their relationships with their spouses, so such a strategy is not without difficulty.

If they plan to have children, aspirants need to consider their feelings about time spent with them. To be a full-time partner and mother requires very good child care and a willingness to hand over much of the rearing of one's children to others. Such child care is expensive, but partners are well remunerated and can afford it. To remain as a partner with family commitments, aspirants can reflect that it is much easier as a partner to put in place arrangements that give flexibility about leaving the office for specific child-related events and it may be possible, in years to come, to be a part-time partner.

An aspirant needs to be prepared to balance the considerable financial and career rewards deriving from partnership with the costs of:

- Reduced engagement with the rearing of her family
- Dilution of the potential richness of the relationship with her spouse
- The possibility of having to defer motherhood until it is too late
- Insufficient time to engage in a range of activities outside of work; and
- High stress levels.

The Elite Women

The women who participated in this study are intelligent and successful. It is presumptuous to suggest how such women might manage things differently. An analysis of their responses, however, suggests some areas for them to consider. The observations are divided into:

- areas for personal reflection;
- areas for possible personal action; and
- ways in which they might contribute to the future development of the firm to facilitate a better gender balance.

Areas for personal reflection

The women work extremely long hours and have to schedule their days carefully, prioritising demands on their time. Mostly, they have little time for themselves and for their relationship with their spouses. They have enormous demands on their time and many spoke of the lack of time to reflect on the path their lives were taking. It is possible that, for some, if not all, it would be useful to do some structured thinking, with a mentor or counsellor who could facilitate such reflection on themselves, their self-esteem, their life priorities and where they want their careers to take them. In this context, it might prove beneficial to see partnership as the beginning of a new career phase, rather than the culmination of their major career objective. It may prove helpful to reflect on their characteristics and their natural and acquired skills and competencies and on their leadership style. This reflection may lead them to a more transformational leadership style instead of assuming the transactional role model discussed in Chapter 3, developed by their mainly male predecessors and peers.

Many of them had huge expectations of themselves and set themselves very high personal goals. They recognised that they expected themselves to be 'superwomen'. Although they accepted that it is not realistic to try to be excellent at everything, they still compared themselves with people who were individually excellent in the various aspects of life achievements. They spoke of the three-stranded lives they lived in terms of their temporal boundaries. They tried to make time for

- their career
- others (children, spouses, families and friends) and
- themselves.

It was as if they wanted to be excellent in all three elements of their lives. However, in assessing themselves, they compared themselves with people who excelled at one of these. So, in relation to their careers, their comparators were partners (usually male) who devoted most of their time to the job and had the support of wives who managed their family and social lives for them. In relation to their time for others, they compared themselves with full-time mothers. In relation to their time for themselves, they compared themselves to friends who did not have heavy family or job commitments and so managed to find lots of time to have their hair done, play tennis, go to plays, have lunch with friends, keep fit and generally look after themselves. So, instead of using a role model who was, like themselves, managing three very demanding jobs, they used an aggregate triumvirate who were respectively managing only one of the three elements. This seemed to me to be an unreasonably tough hurdle for them to overcome and one that might warrant some reflection.

Areas for personal action

There are relatively few elite women in the accountancy profession and, until a critical mass is reached, being a pioneer can be a lonely station. There have been some efforts to establish a network for women at the top of the profession, with mixed success. The participants to this study tended to resist the idea of establishing or joining a women's network. There were several reasons for this. Some did not wish to be seen as 'girlie'; some felt that it would absorb precious time and some had not considered the possibility.

Another possible explanation is that, since many of the women display masculine characteristics, they may not identify immediately with the idea of a women's network. However, it would appear, from this study, that there are many common issues for the elite women to share and discuss and establishing a network would be a good forum for sharing and understanding experiences. This may be an area where a cross-firm initiative may prove fruitful, and where common ideas and solutions could have considerable pay-back for all parties and for the profession, but particularly for the women themselves.

Powerful mentoring is significant in attaining partnership. However, the impact of mentoring is mediated by a series of significant variables, which include gender. Women partners have the capacity to be significant role models, to offer social support and to assist the career development of female protégées and yet they are not actively engaging in same-gender mentoring. This can be explained by their own experience of male mentors, their sense of lack of training in the area of mentoring and their awareness that mentoring does not directly earn fees. Women partners could usefully consider changing this situation by working with their partners to enhance the value placed on mentoring, by establishing a mentoring training programme and actively undertaking the mentoring of women and men with feminine characteristics on the partnership track.

Areas for contributing to change in the firm

There are several ways in which the elite women can raise the awareness of their fellow partners. This includes helping to change the culture of the firm from, as described by some of the women, 'blokey' to one that is more diverse, in which people are comfortable displaying feminine as well as masculine characteristics. This issue of firm culture is subtle and does mean producing a list of 'Dos' and 'Don'ts', such as banning risqué stories or stipulating politically correct behaviour such as not assuming that the woman present at the meeting will automatically take the minutes or pour the tea. Rather it offers powerful women the opportunity to raise awareness of how they feel about the way business is done and, hopefully for men, to keep their antennae raised to detect the subtle differences in the way decisions are made and executed. It also includes debating the possibility of part-time working and flexible working for partners, and supporting other women partners who bring 'girlie' issues to partners' meetings or who seek to use a more transformational style.

THE BIG FOUR FIRMS

This research permits conclusions on the mechanisms used for selecting partners and structuring the partnership track. The current model has not achieved a good gender balance at the top of the firms. It was explained in Chapter 2 that the accountancy profession was designed by men to accommodate men, and common sense tells us that change cannot be effected overnight by producing a magic 'to do' list. However, there are some lessons that emerge from this research that could increase awareness and accelerate the process of promoting more women to partnership level.

A male culture

The elite women did not identify overt gender discrimination in the firms. Indeed, current legislation would make such discrimination highly unlikely. However, this research suggests that the culture in the firms is masculine. Firm culture is an ephemeral area, and difficult to measure with any level of accuracy. However, the culture in the Big Four firms was described by the elite women as being 'blokey', or male and characterised by activities such as networking, drinking, golf, talking about sport and behaviours that are generally associated with men. Anything perceived as 'girly' was not as well understood. In order to be elected to partnership and to stay in that role, women have to fit into that culture and to display or learn to display more masculine than feminine characteristics. The study does not establish whether the elite women possessed a high level of masculine characteristics before they entered the accountancy profession or learned to behave in a masculine way in response to the environment. Either way, the research suggests that women displaying predominantly masculine characteristics are favoured when electing partners. The literature suggests that women displaying feminine characteristics use a more transformational than transactional style of leadership. So, although the style that women generally adopt (for example, inclusion, consultation and people orientation) is increasingly recognised and valued in business, it does not seem to be specifically valued in electing partners in the Big Four firms.

For example, many of the women whom I interviewed felt that it was assumed that women would be better as HR partners and in dealing with the staff counselling areas. However, this may not be a valid assumption if the women partners are expected to be masculine or to adopt masculine characteristics. The elite women themselves expressed a reluctance to gravitate towards these roles since they are not highly valued within the firm. In spite of lip service being paid towards nurturing staff, the indicator of a successful partner is essentially fee-earning capacity. Firms should consider an affirmative action policy of retaining and promoting more women (and men) with predominantly feminine characteristics. It would seem that they could usefully engage in a process of understanding and valuing the different management styles that people with feminine characteristics can bring to the firm. They could also ensure that their performance review systems really value and reward non-chargeable activities that contribute indirectly to the value of the partnership.

The partnership track

The partnership track has changed over the period covered by the experience of the elite women who participated in this study. It has moved from a penumbral system characterised by cloning, favouritism and self-marketing by the candidate to a more transparent system with more objective performance reviews and the use of independent assessment centres and allocated counselling mentors. In such an environment of change and development, it is normal to find that there is still room for improvement. The outcome of the current process is that the women who successfully travel the partnership track tend to have come from single-sex schools, have graduated with very good degrees in business, finance, law or related subjects and have, since qualification, remained in the firm with a short secondment to enhance their experience. They feel that they have to be better than their male counterparts to compete successfully but are uncomfortable about marketing their own successes. They all have a very high level of commitment to the firm and work extremely long hours.

This homogeneity, in conjunction with the point made about the masculinity of the elite women, should lead the firms to reflect on the partnership track process. It may be appropriate to identify and track some more women who

- have come from non-traditional backgrounds;
- have non-business degrees;
- come directly from another Big Four firm or from industry;
- are not willing to be present for the excessive hours demanded but may be willing to take a lower profit share; or
- have 'softer' skills and competencies with a capacity to develop transformational leadership.

Additionally, this study suggests that the assessment mechanisms built into the partnership track process could take into account the different way that women market their successes and failures. Only by making the partnership track a process where people with masculine and feminine characteristics are equally likely to succeed will the firms begin to enhance their diversity at the top.

A mentoring system

There seems little doubt about the importance of an effective mentoring experience. It would appear that mentoring systems are becoming more organised and formal in the Big Four firms. However, as with all personal relationships, formal standard operating procedures will not necessarily produce a happy outcome. Research has found that mentoring in accountancy firms comprises three elements: career development, social support and role modelling. The elite women in this study identified elements of all three in their mentoring experiences, although they favoured an informal system where chemistry drove the establishment of the mentoring relationship. However, informal mentoring has the potential for inequity if mentors and protégées are simply allowed to mutually self-select. They all identified the importance of having a male mentor and few of them saw themselves as having a specific role in mentoring young women themselves. This is connected to the preponderance of male characteristics present in the female partners. Mentoring is complex and dynamic and can be either fruitful or damaging, which is understandable given that it is a human relationship embracing the three-way involvement of mentor, protégée and firm in the highly charged process of the partnership track. Since the relationship between mentor and protégée is so significant in the achievement of partnership, it is suggested that policies and procedures in this area, particularly the issues of equity in informal mentoring; the possibility of different types of mentoring systems at various points on the career track; and the role of female mentors for potential female candidates in providing role modelling, are fertile areas for the firms to explore and develop.

Reward models

The elite women who participated in this study described the reward system as one in which commitment to the firm and willingness to devote very long and unsociable hours to serving the needs of the client and the firm are rewarded by high-level profit share. Part-time partnerships are not a normal feature of the system. The women partners felt that it does not work well because part-time partners drift towards full-time working but with a part-time profit share and a weakening of their voice at partnership decision-making fora. Other partners resent the fact that someone else has to take up the slack when they are out of the office. However, there was a desire, expressed both by women with family commitments and women who are approaching retirement, for an acceptable standard policy of part-time partnership rather than an ad hoc arrangement for a small minority. The women partners enjoy the financial rewards and the financial independence conferred by the present model. However, the implication of this study for the firms is that there is a hunger for the development of the reward system which offers a choice of financial and other rewards (for example, longer holidays; shorter days, part-time working and other flexible working arrangements).

Partnership development

This study indicates that elite women feel that the partnership track is like a ride on a powerful wave, with an external force driving the direction and undulations of the wave. They themselves have to paddle strongly and exercise skill to stay on the wave, and if they make no mistakes, the wave will land them on the golden beach of partnership. Once on the beach, the partners spoke of a sense of withdrawal of the external force and a sense of being on their own in progressing their career path from that point. While the partners themselves have a pivotal role in managing their post-partnership career, there appears to be a lacuna in the support offered by the firm to its partners. Women partners expressed an unwillingness to engage in the political arena of partnership leadership. This is surprising given their levels of competitiveness and masculinity. However, it may be explained by their decision to focus on having a family and balancing their time between family and the job. Mounting a campaign to be Group Partner or Managing Partner or to join the Policy Committee would involve significant time commitment which they could ill-afford at a time they are starting a family. Additionally, it would involve a high level of networking and establishing alliances – including the possibility of making some enemies. These are areas which the elite women described as unattractive and that may also explain their reluctance to forward their post-partnership careers in this way. The outcome of this decision is that the very top of these firms is even more male-dominated and the chances of a diverse leadership style are even slimmer.

The Big Four Firms have excellent training schemes in place for staff at all levels to deal with technical issues and other areas relating to their jobs. However, it would seem from this study that the partner development programme could be strengthened to support partners in developing the additional skills and competencies necessary for leadership including people management, counselling, networking (including support for a Women's Network), stress management, mentoring and so on. Such a development programme could usefully be planned over the post-partnership career of the partner. It could also, at an appropriate juncture, incorporate planning for retirement to support the partner's sense of worth and dignity, but also to ensure that the firm manages the difficult balance between benefiting from the 'grey head' competencies of the pre-retirement partner while effecting smooth succession planning.

CONCLUSION

To sum up, it can be concluded that there are some common themes that can be identified in the success stories of elite women in accountancy. Women experience difficulties that men do not in attaining and retaining elite positions within the accountancy profession. The most positive way of formulating strategies to address this breakdown of equality is to lay down positive steps to be taken in order to achieve gender equality. Of course, gender equality is recognised as a principle in international law, dating back to the 1984 Declaration of Human Rights and subsequently supported by national equality legislation. However, when there is a long-standing and deeply entrenched system of male dominance in a particular sphere of human activity, effecting change requires more than a change in the law.

The opening up of the higher echelons of the accountancy profession to women requires a change in complex norms that have been established. They include patterns of power relationships, economic and reward arrangements, emotional responses, and systems of communication and meaning. Change requires that the issue is placed on the firms' agendae and that women themselves work towards understanding the environment in which they work and accept that change often happens in an evolutionary rather than revolutionary way. Women are working to achieve a critical mass at all levels of work and still have much to do. Women in elite positions have a role to play in redefining the workplace to make it more congruent with women's own objectives. However, the men are also involved in the process of understanding and change. They are largely the people who control the resources, the political power and the cultural authority and they must also engage with the process of change. Additionally, a significant force for change must come from women with predominantly female characteristics, who feel comfortable displaying those characteristics and who are rewarded for the skills and competencies they bring to the firms in the same way as those who display male characteristics.

REFERENCES AND FURTHER READING

Acker J. (1990), Hierarchies, jobs, bodies: A theory of gendered organisation, *Gender and Society* 4, pp 139–158.

Alimo-Metcalfe, B. (1998), *Are there gender and cultural differences in constructs of transformational leadership?*, Presented to 24th International Conference of Applied Psychology, San Francisco, CA.

Alimo-Metcalfe, B. and Alban-Metcalfe J. (2003), *Leadership: a Masculine Past, but a Feminine Future?*, Paper presented to the annual BPS Occupational Psychology Conference, August 2003.

Ashburner (1994), Women in Management Careers: Opportunities and Outcomes in Evetts J. (ed), *Women and Career: Themes and Issues in Advanced Industrial Societies*.

Avolio B. J., Bass B., and Jung D. (1999), Re-examining the Components of transformational and Transactional Leadership using the Multifactor leadership questionnaire, *Journal of Occupational and Organizational Psychology*, Vol. 72, pp 441–62.

Bacik I, Costello, C. and E. Drew (2003), *Gender Injustice*, Trinity College Dublin Law School, Dublin.

Bagihole B. (2002), *Women in Non-Traditional Occupations – Challenging Men*, Palgrave MacMillan, Basingstoke.

Banner L. W. (1983), *American Beauty*, Knopf, New York.

Barker P. (1988), The True and Fair Sex, in Rowe D. (ed.), *The Irish Chartered Accountant: Centenary Essays*, Gill & Macmillan, Dublin.

Barker P. and Monks K. (1998), Irish Women Accountants and Career Progression, *Accounting, Organizations and Society* Vol. 23, No. 8, pp 813–823.

Barker P. and Monks K. (2003), *Leadership Style and Women: Two Cases*, Proceedings of Third European Conference on Gender Equality, Genoa, March.

Becker H., and Geer H. (1957), Participant Observation and Interviewing: A Comparison, *Human Organization*, 16 (3): pp 28–32.

Bell E., and Bryman A. (2007), The Ethics of Management Research: An Exploratory Content Analysis, *British Journal of Management*, 18 (1): pp 63–77.

Bem. S. L. (1975), Sex-role Adaptability: One consequence of Psychological Androgyny, *Journal of Personality and Social Psychology*, Vol. 31, pp 634–43.

Bennett L. (1935), *Report of his meeting to IWWU*, Executive Minutes, September 5, 1935.

Booth M. (1996), Women as Lawyers, in *Women and Higher Education, Past, Present and Future*, Masson M. and Simonton D. (eds), pp 267–273, University of Aberdeen Press, Aberdeen.

Bertaux D. (1981) (ed.), Biography and society: The Life History Approach in *Social Sciences*, Sage, London.

Brenner O. C. (1982), Relationship of Education to Sex, Managerial Status, and the Managerial Stereotype, *Journal of Applied Psychology*, Vol. 67, pp 380–8.

Brewer N, Mitchell, P., and Weber N. (2002), Gender Role, Organizational Status and Conflict Management Styles, *International Journal of Conflict Management*, Vol. 13, Issue 1, pp 78–95.

Brodsky M. (1993), Successful Female Corporate Managers and Entrepreneurs: Similarities and Differences, *Group and Organization Management*, 18(3).

Bryman A. (1988), *Quantity and Quality in Social Research*, Unwin Hyman, London.

Bulmer M. (1988), *Doing Research in Organisations*, Routledge, London.

Burgess R. G. (1982), *Field Research: A Source Book and Field Manual*, Allen & Unwin, London.

Burstyn J. (1973), Education and Sex: The Medical Case against Higher Education for Women in England, 1870–1890, in *Proceedings of the American Philosophical Society*, Vol. 117, pp 79–89.

Butler J. (1990), *Gender Trouble: Feminism and the Subversion of Identity*, Routledge, London.

Butler P. (1981), *Self Assertion for Women*, Harper and Row, San Francisco.

Carr-Saunders, A. M. and Wilson, P. A. (1933), *The Professions*, Oxford: Oxford University Press, 1933.

Cathro L. (1995), More than Just Stories: Narrative Enquiry in Research, *Education Research and Perspectives*, Vol. 22, No. 1, pp 53–65.

Charles N. (1993), *Gender Divisions and Social Change*, Harvester-Wheatsheaf.

Chua W. F. and Clegg S. (1990), Professional Closure: The Case of British Nursing, *Theory and Society* (1990) pp 135–172.

Cockburn C. (1991), In *the Way of Women*, Palgrave Macmillan, London.

Collins K. (1993), Stress and Departures from the Public Accounting Profession: A Study of Gender Differences, *Accounting Horizons*, March, Vol. 7, No 1, pp 29–38.

Constitution of the Irish Free State (Saorstát Éireann) Act, 1922; No. 1/1922.

Corlett A. B. (1873), Letter to Provost and Board at Trinity College, Dublin Library, College Muniments, P/1/2153.

CPA Editorial (2003), Women Hold 13.2% of Large Firm Partnerships, *CPA Personnel Report*, Vol. 22. No. 10.

Cullen M. (1985), *How Radical was Irish Feminism Between 1860 and 1920?*

Dalton D. and Hill J. (1997), Women as Managers and Partners, *Auditing*, Spring, Vol. 16, Issue 1, pp 29–53.

Daly L. (1902), Women and the University Question, *New Ireland Review*, Vol. 17, 1902.

Daly M. (1981), Women in the Irish Workforce from Pre-Industrial to Modern Times, in *Saothar 7*.

Davidson M and Cooper C. (1992), *Shattering the Glass Ceiling: The Woman Manager*, Paul Chapman, London.

De Beauvoir S. (1949), *La Deuxieme Sexe*, translated (1953), Parshley H. M., David Campbell Publishers, London, p. 281.

Donnell S. M., and Hall J. (1980) Men and Women as Managers: a Significant Case of no Significant Difference, *Organizational Dynamics*, Spring pp 60–77.

Downes M. (1888), *The Case of the Catholic Lady Students of the Royal University Stated*, cited in Raftery and Parkes (2007).

Diem-Willie G. and Ziegler J. (2000), Traditional and New Ways of Living, in *Gendering Elites*, Vianello and Moore, Macmillan Press, Basingstoke.

Drew, E., Moore G., Siemienska R and M. Vianello (2000), A Theoretical Framework, in *Gendering Elites*, Vianello and Moore, Macmillan Press, Basingstoke.

Duncker, P. (1999), *James Miranda Barry*, Serpent's Tail, London.

Eagly A., Johannesen-Schmidt and M. van Engen (2003), Transformational, Transactional and Laissez-Faire Leadership Styles: A Meta-Analysis Comparing Women and Men, *Psychological Bulletin*, Vol. 129, No. 4, pp 569–591.

Eagly A. H. (2007), Female Leadership Advantage and Disadvantage: Resolving the Contradictions, *Psychology of Women Quarterly*, 31, pp 1–12.

Easterby-Smith M., Thorpe, R & P. Jackson (2008), *Management Research*, Sage Publications, London.

Edinburgh Review (1810), Rights and Conditions of Women, *Edinburgh Review* 73, January 1841.

Edwards J. (1989), *A History of Financial Accounting*, Routledge, London.

Elliott, P. (1972), *The Sociology of the Professions*, London: Macmillan Press, 1972.

Ellis S. (1845), *The Daughters of England*, London: Fortescue Press.

Ely R. (1994), The Social Construction of Relationships among Professional Women at Work, in Davidson M., and Burke R. (eds.) *Women in Management, Current Research Issues*, Paul Chapman: London.

Evans, R. J. (1977), *The Feminists: Women's Emancipation Movements in Europe, America and Australasia 1840–1920*, London.

Faludi S. (1991), *Backlash: The undeclared war against American Women*, New York: Crown Publishers.

Ferrarotti F. (1981), On the Autonomy of the Biographical Method, in Dertaux D. (ed.), *Biography and Society*, Sage, London.

Finn I. (1955), Women in the Medical Profession in Ireland, 1876–1919, in Whelan B. (ed.), *Women and Paid Work in Ireland, 1500–1930*, Four Courts Press, Dublin.

Fordyce J. (1794), *Sermons to Young Women*, 1:24, 26, 213, London: Millar, W. Law & R. Cater.

Fisher C. and Lovell A. (2006), *Business Ethics and Values*, Pearson Education-Prentice Hall: Harlow, Essex.

Freidson E. (1970), *Professional Dominance: The Social Structure of Medical Care*, Atherton Press, New York.

Gaskell, E. (1967), *The Letters of Mrs Gaskell*, Chapple J. A and Pollard A. (eds), Cambridge, Mass: Harvard University Press.

Gisborne T. (1798), *An Enquiry into the Duties of the Female Sex*, Philadelphia: James Humphreys.

Gordon S. (1991), *Prisoners of Men's Dreams: Striking Out for a New Feminine Future*, Boston: Little, Brown.

Garcia-Retamero R. and Lopez-Zafra E. (2006), Prejudice against Women in Male-Congenial Environments: Perceptions of Gender Role Congruity in Leadership, *Sex Roles*, 55, pp 51–61.

Greenhalgh T. Russell J. D. Swinglehurst, (2005), Narrative Methods in Quality Improvement Research, *Quality & Safety in Health Care*, 14(6):443–449, December 2005.

Gregory J. (1774), *A Father's Legacy to His Daughters*, pp 6–7, 52, New York: Garland Publishing, 1974.

Hall V. (1996), *Dancing on the Ceiling: A Study of Women Managers in Education*, Chapman Publishing Ltd, London.

Hammond, T. and Streeter, D. W. (1994), Overcoming Barriers: Early African-American Certified Public Accountants, *Accounting, Organizations and Society*, pp 271–288.

Hammond, T. (1996), *Oral Testimony and the History of African-American Accountants: The Narratives of Theodora Rutherford, Lincoln Harrison and Richard Austin,*

Paper presented at the 19th Annual Congress of the European Accounting Association, Bergen, 1996.

Harding A. (1995), Elite Theory and Growth Machines, in *Theories of Urban Politics*, Judge, D., Stoker, G., and F. Wolman Sage Publications London. pp 35–54.

Haythornthwaite A. (2003), One in Eleven, *Accountancy*, July 2003, Vol. 132.

Healy M., and Rawlinson M. (1994), Interviewing Techniques in Business and Management Research, in Wass V. and Wells P. (eds), *Principles and Practice in Business and Management Research*, Dartmouth Publishing Company, Aldershot.

Heard M. (2003), Barriers for Women Continue to Lessen, *CPA Personnel Report, October 2003*, p. 3.

Hirschmann L. (2006), *Get to Work: A manifesto for women of the world*, Penguin Books: New York.

Hobsbawm E. J. (1962), *The Age of Revolution 1789–1848*, New American Library: New York.

Holland J. (1997), *Making Vocational Choices*, Englewood Cliffs, NJ: Prentice Hall.

Holt C. (1998), Assessing the Current Validity of the Bem Sex-Role Inventory, *Sex Roles*, December 1998.

Hopfl H. and Sumahon M. (2007), "The Lady Vanishes": Some thoughts on Women and Leadership, *Journal of Organizational Change Management*, Vol. 20, No. 2, pp 198–208.

Hughes, E. C., *Men and their Work*, Glencoe, Illinois: Free Press, 1958.

Institute of Chartered Accountants (2008), *Annual Report of the Institute of Chartered Accountants in Ireland*.

Jackson C. (2002), Can Single-Sex Classes in Co-Educational Schools Enhance the Learning Experiences of Girls and/or Boys? *British Educational Research Journal*, Vol. 28, No. 1 (Feb., 2002), pp 37–48.

Kark R. (2004), The Transformational Leader: who is s/he?: A Feminist Perspective, *Journal of Organizational Change Management*, 17, 2, pp 160–174.

Kirkham, L. M. and Loft, A. (1993), Gender and the Construction of the Professional Accountant, *Accounting, Organizations and Society* (1993), pp 507–558.

Knights D. and Odin P. (1995), "It's about time!" The Significance of Gendered Time for Financial Services Consumption, *Time and Society*, 4(2): 205–31.

Koberg C. S., Boss R.W. and Goodman E. (1998), Factors and Outcomes Associated with Mentoring, *Journal of Vocational Behaviour*, 53 (1), pp 55–72.

Kristeva J. (1981), *Women's Time* in *Feminisms*, Warhol R. and Herndl D. (eds) (1997), New Brunswick: Rutgers University Press.

Kulik L. (2000), Jobless men and women: A comparative analysis of job search intensity, attitudes towards unemployment, *Journal of Occupational and Organizational Psychology*, 73, 487–500.

Larson, M. S. *The Rise of Professionalism, A Sociological Analysis,* Berkeley: University of California Press, 1977.

Lee J.J. (1978), Women and the Church since the Famine, in MacCurtain M. and O Corrain D. (eds), *Women in Irish Society: The Historical Dimension,* Dublin.

Liddle J. and Michielsens E. (2000), Gender, Class and Public Power, in *Gendering Elites,* Vianello and Moore, Macmillan Press, Basingstoke.

Lievens F., Decaesteker C., Coestsier P. and J. Geirnaert (2001), Organisational attractiveness for prospective applicants, *Applied Psychology: An International Review,* 50, 30–51.

Loden M. (1985), *Feminine Leadership, or How to Succeed in Business without Being One of the Boys,* Times Books, London.

Lowe K., Kroeck K. and Sivasubramaniam N. (1996), Effectiveness of correlates of Transformational and Transactional Leadership: a Meta-analytic review of the MLQ Literature, *Leadership Quarterly,* Vol. 7, pp 385–425.

Luddy M. (2000), Women and Work in Nineteenth and early Twentieth Century Ireland, in *Women and Paid Work in Ireland 1500–1930,* Whelan B. ed., Four Courts Press, Dublin.

Lyotard, J. F. (1989), One of the Things at Stake in Women's Struggles, in Benjamin A., (ed.), The *Lyotard Reader,* pp 111–121, Basil Blackwell: Oxford.

McCarthy Helen (2004), *Girlfriends in High Places? How Women's Networks are Changing the Workplace,* Demos, London.

Macdonald, K. M. *The Sociology of the Professions,* London: Sage, 1995.

Marshall J. (1993), Organisational Cultures and Women Managers: Exploring the Dynamics of Resiliance, *Applied Psychology: An International Review,* 424, pp 313–322.

Marshall J. (1995), *Women Managers Moving On: Exploring Career and Life Choices,* Routledge, London.

Melucci A. (1996), *The Playing Self: Person and Meaning in the Planetary Society,* Cambridge University Press.

Messengill D. and Dimarco N. (1979), Sex-role Stereotypes and Requisite Management Characteristics: A current replication, *Sex Roles,* Vol. 5, pp 561–70.

Metcalf B., and Linstead A. (2003), Gendering Teamwork: Re-Writing the Feminine, *Gender Work and Organization,* Vol. 10, No. 1.

Mill J. S. (1869), The Subjection of Women, cited in *The Feminists,* Evans R. J. (ed.) Croom Helm: London (1977).

Miller J. (1976), *Towards a New Psychology of Women,* Beacon Press, Boston.

Murphy M. (1955), Recent Research in Business Accounting History, *The Business History Review,* Vol. 29, No. 3. (Sep. 1955), pp 263–276.

Newton J. (1981), Women's Time in Feminisms, Warhol R. and Herndl D. eds (1997), New Brunswick: Rutgers University Press.

Nicholson V. (2008), *Singled Out*, Penguin Books, London.

Oakley J. (2000), Gender-based Barriers to Senior Management Positions, *Journal of Business Ethics*, 27: pp 321–334.

O'Connor V. (2001), Women and Men in Senior Management – a "Different Needs" Hypothesis, *Women in Management Review*, Vol. 16, No. 8, pp 400–404.

O'hOgartaigh M. (2000), Nurses and Midwives in Ireland in the Early Twentieth Century, in *Women and Paid Work in Ireland 1500–1930*, Whelan B., (ed.) Four Courts Press, Dublin.

Owens R. C. (2005), *A Social History of Women in Ireland 1870–1970*, Gill & Macmillan, Dublin.

Palgi M. (2000), Top People and Mentors, in *Gendering Elites*, Vianello and Moore, Macmillan Press, Basingstoke.

Parasuraman S. and Greenhaus J. H. (1993), *Personal portrait: The Life Style of the Woman Manager*, in Fagenson E. A. (ed.), *Women in Management*, Sage, pp 186–211.

Parkin F. (1979), *Marxism and Class Theory, A Bourgeois Critique*, Tavistock, London.

Pearson A. (2002), *I don't know how she does it*, Alfred A. Knopf: New York.

Pedlar M, Burgoyne, M. and T. Boydell (2004), *A Manager's Guide to Leadership*, McGraw Hill, London.

Peiss K. (1998), *Hope in a Jar: the Making of America's Beauty Culture*, Metropolitan Books, New York.

Perriton, L. (2007), Forgotten Feminists: the Federation of British Professional and Business Women 1933–1969, *Women's History Review*, No. 16:1, pp 79–97.

Raferty D., and Parkes S. (2007), *Female Education in Ireland 1700–1900*, Irish Academic Press, Dublin.

Ramli A. (2002), *Challenges Facing the Women Accountants in the New Millenium*, Akauntan Nasioinal, May 2002.

Redmond M. (2002), The Emergence of Women in the Solicitors' Profession in Ireland, in Hall E., and Hogan D. (eds.), *The Law Society of Ireland 1852–2002*, Four Courts Press, Dublin.

Richardson, A. J. (1989), Canada's Accounting Elite: 1880–1930, *The Accounting Historians Journal* (1989) pp 1–21.

Richardson A. P. (1923), Editorial in the *Journal of Accountancy*, December 1923.

Roberts J and Coutts A. (1992), Feminization and Professionalization: a review of an emerging literature on the development of accounting in the United Kingdom, *Accounting, Organizations and Society*, pp 379–395.

Rosen B. and Jerdee T. (1978), Perceived Sex Differences in Managerially Relevant Characteristics, *Sex Roles*, Vol. 4, pp 837–43.

Rosener J. (1995), *America's Competitive Secret: Women Managers*, Oxford University Press: New York.

Rosener J. (1990), Ways Women Lead, *Harvard Business Review,* Nov/Dec.

Rosenthal P. (1995), Gender Differences in Managers – Attributions for Successful Work Performance, *Women in Management Review,* Vol. 10, No. 6, pp 26–31.

Royal Commission on University Education (Ireland) – the Robertson Commission – (1903), Final Report [Cd. 1483-4] xxxii.i, Minutes of Evidence, p. 391.

Sayer A. and Morgan K. (1985), A Modern Industry in a Delcining Region: Links between Method, Theory and Policy, in D. Massey and R Meegan (eds), *Politics and Method: Contrasting Studies in Industrial Geography,* Methuen: London.

Scandura T. and Viator R. (1994), Mentoring in Public Accounting Firms: An Analysis of Mentor-Protégé Relationships, *Accounting, Organisations and Society* 19(8), pp 717–734.

Schein V. (1973), The Relationship between Sex Role Stereotypes and Requisite Management Characteristics, *Journal of Applied Psychology,* Vol. 57, pp 95–100.

Schneider B. (1987), The People make the Place, *Personnel Psychology,* 40, 437–453.

Schwartz F. (1998), Management Women and the New Facts of Life, *Harvard Business Review,* Jan/Feb, pp 65–76.

Seneca Declaration (1848), printed in William L. O'Neill, *The Woman Movement: Feminism in the United States and England,* London, 1969, pp 108–11.

Seron C. and Ferris K. (1995), Negotiating Professionalism: the Gendered Social Capital of Felxible Time, *Work and Occupations,* 22(1): 22–47.

Shaw C. (1966), *The Jack Roller,* 2nd Ed., University of Chicago Press: Chicago.

Sheppard D. L. (1989), Organizations, Power and Sexuality: the Image and Self-image of Women Managers, in Hearn J., Sheppard D. L., Tancred-Sherrif P. and G. Burrell (eds), *The Sexuality of Organizations,* Sage Publications, London, pp 139–157.

Simonton D. (1998), *A History of European Women's Work – 1700 to Present,* Routledge, London.

Sinclair, A. (1999), *Doing Leadership Differently,* Melbourne University Press, Australia.

Steinberg R. and Shapiro S. (1982), Sex differences in Personality Traits of Female and Male Master of Business Administration Students, *Journal of Applied Psychology,* Vol. 67, pp 306–10.

Stone P. (2007), *Opting Out? Why Women Really Quit Careers and Head Home,* University of California Press, Berkeley.

Stone P. and Kuperberg A. (2005), *The New Feminine Mystique: A content analysis of the print media depiction of women who exchange careers for motherhood,* Paper presented at the annual meeting of the Eastern Sociological Society, Washington DC.

Swasy A. (1993), Status Symbols: Stay at home moms are fashionable again, *Wall Street Journal,* July 23:A1, Column 1.

Tagg S. (1985), Life Story Interviews and Their Interpretations, in Brenner M., Brown J., and D. Canter (eds), *The Research Interview – Uses and Approaches*, Academic Press, Harcourt Brace Jovanovich: London.

Ticehurst G., and Veal A. (2000), *Business Research Methods*, Longman, Australia.

Tishler L. (2004), Where are the Women? *Fast Company*, Feb., Issue 79, p. 52–58.

Tod I. M. S. (1873), The Education of Women, *Journal of the Women's Education Union*, 1, 1873.

Tod I. M. S. (1874), On the Education of Girls of the Middle Classes, London, in Luddy M. (ed.) *Women in Ireland, 1800–1918: A Documentary History*, Cork, 1996, pp 108–110.

Turner B. (1987), *Medical Power and Social Knowledge*, Sage, London.

Van Vianen A., and Fischer A. (2002), Illuminating the Glass Ceiling, the Role of Organizational Culture Preferences, *Journal of Occupational & Organizational Psychology*, September, Vol. 75, Issue 3, pp 315–338.

Wajcman J. (1998), *Managing like a Man*, Polity Press: Cambridge.

Walby S. (1997), *Theorizing Patriarchy*, Basil Blackwell: Oxford.

Walker R. (1985), *Applied Quantitative Research*, Gower: Aldershot.

Walsh M. (1992), Plush Endeavours: an Analysis of the Modern American Soft-toy Industry, *Business History Review*, No. 66, Winter, pp 637–670.

Wass V. J. and Wells P. (1994), *Principles and Practice in Business and Management Research*, Dartmouth Publishing Company: Aldershot.

Wellington S., Kroof, M and Gerkovich P. (2003), What is holding Women Back? *Harvard Business Review*, June, Vol. 81, Issue 6, pp 18–21.

White B., Cox C., and Cooper, C L. (1997), A Portrait of Successful Women, *Women in Management Review*, Vol. 12, No. 1, pp 27–34.

Willett J. A. (2000), *Permanent Waves, the Making of the American Beauty Shop*, New York University Press: New York.

Woodward A. and Lyon D. (2000), Gendered Time and Women's Access to Power, in *Gendering Elites*, Vianello and Moore, Macmillan Press, Basingstoke.

Woolf V. (1931), Professions for Women, in Leaska M., *The Pargiters*, New York Public Library and Readex Books: New York (1977).